OH WHAT A
SLAUGHTER

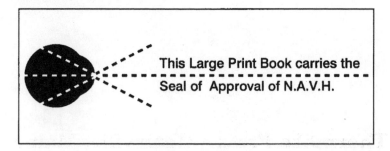

This Large Print Book carries the
Seal of Approval of N.A.V.H.

OH WHAT A SLAUGHTER

MASSACRES IN THE AMERICAN WEST
1846-1890

LARRY McMURTRY

Thorndike Press • Waterville, Maine

Published in 2006 by arrangement with
Simon & Schuster, Inc.

Thorndike Press® Large Print Americana.

The tree indicium is a trademark of Thorndike Press.

The text of this Large Print edition is unabridged.
Other aspects of the book may vary from the original edition.

Set in 16 pt. Plantin.

Printed in the United States on permanent paper.

Library of Congress Cataloging-in-Publication Data

McMurtry, Larry.
    Oh what a slaughter : massacres in the American West,
    1846–1890 / by Larry McMurtry. — Large print ed.
        p. cm.
    Includes bibliographical references.
    ISBN 0-7862-8378-5 (lg. print : hc : alk. paper)
    1. Indians of North America — Wars — West (U.S.)
    2. Indians of North America — West (U.S.) — History —
    19th century.   3. Massacres — West (U.S.) — History —
    19th century.   I. Title.
    E78.W5M35 2006
    973.04′97078—dc22   2005033813

OH WHAT A SLAUGHTER

As the Founder/CEO of NAVH, the only national health agency solely devoted to those who, although not totally blind, have an eye disease which could lead to serious visual impairment, I am pleased to recognize Thorndike Press* as one of the leading publishers in the large print field.

Founded in 1954 in San Francisco to prepare large print textbooks for partially seeing children, NAVH became the pioneer and standard setting agency in the preparation of large type.

Today, those publishers who meet our standards carry the prestigious "Seal of Approval" indicating high quality large print. We are delighted that Thorndike Press is one of the publishers whose titles meet these standards. We are also pleased to recognize the significant contribution Thorndike Press is making in this important and growing field.

Lorraine H. Marchi, L.H.D.
Founder/CEO
NAVH

* Thorndike Press encompasses the following imprints: Thorndike, Wheeler, Walker and Large Print Press.

Contents

Comes the most heartrending tale of all. As I have said Before General Custer with five companies went below the village to cut them off as he supposed but instead he was surrounded and all of them killed to a man 14 officers and 250 men There the bravest general of modder times met his death with his two brothers, brotherinlaw and nephew not 5 yards apart, surrounded by 42 men of E Company. Oh what a slaughter how many homes made desolate by the sad disaster everyone of them were scalped and otherwise mutilated but the General he lay with a smile on his face.

PRIVATE THOMAS COLEMAN
I Buried Custer

THE

MEAT SHOP

Of "massacre" (the noun) the *OED* suggests "shambles, butchery, general slaughter, carnage," a definition that would probably work for the great scout Kit Carson, who called the 1846 massacre of an undetermined number of California Indians, in which he took part, "a perfect butchery."

Of "massacre" (the verb) the same authority offers "to violently kill, mutilate, mangle," a fair description of what was done to the victims in the course of the various massacres I intend to consider in this book.

The Encyclopaedia Britannica, eleventh edition, allots the subject a hasty paragraph, concluding that — though the word is very obscure — the etymology suggests something like a meat shop: a very bloody place, a shambles, with discarded and undesirable pieces of meat scattered around.

The image of a meat shop seems apt to me, since what massacres usually do is

11

reduce human beings to the condition of meat, though the bits of meat will be less tidily arranged than the cuts would normally be in a decent butcher shop.

If we know anything about man, it's that he's not pacific. The temptation to butcher anyone considered undesirable seems to be a common temptation, not always resisted. The twentieth century, just passed, more or less began with the million-plus massacre of the Armenians by the Turks, and ended with the terrible low-tech chopping up of some 800,000 Tutsis in Rwanda, an old-style massacre mostly accomplished with hoes and hatchets. When it ended a good deal of Rwanda resembled a meat shop.

What I want to do in this book is look at several massacres that occurred in the American West during the several decades when the native tribes of our plains and deserts were being displaced from their traditional territories by a vast influx of white immigrants. This process began in the 1830s, but accelerated sharply in the 1840s and 1850s: it was mostly completed, insofar as the native tribes were concerned, by 1890.

Judged by world-historical perspectives these massacres were tiny. The Custer defeat in 1876, a military encounter that, to the great surprise of the general who was soon to lie dead with a smile on his face, was the only one of these encounters to involve more than two hundred dead, a figure hardly to be counted among the world's huge cruelties. Though I describe here and there some tiny massacres, involving only a handful of people, I am mainly concerned with the famous massacres, with death tolls over one hundred people.

But it should be remembered that the body count in the six massacres I'm especially interested in still adds up to fewer than one thousand people, barely one-third of the number who died in New York and Washington on September 11, 2001.

But places and contexts differ: in the thinly populated West of the nineteenth century the violent extinction of more than one hundred people was no light thing, though a few of the assailants at first pretended that it was. Massacres are not like vast natural disasters: the Galveston Flood, the San Francisco Earthquake, the eruption of Krakatoa.

Massacres require human volition, and the extremes that result not infrequently produce trauma and, sometimes, guilt. Though in most cases the men who did the killings I describe escaped legal retribution, they did not escape the trauma that followed on the terror they inflicted.

Nephi Johnson, one of the participants in the Mountain Meadows Massacre, died crying "Blood, blood, blood!"

Though more than a century has passed since Wounded Knee, the most recent of these massacres, bitterness has yet to leach out of the descendants of those massacred. Very probably one of the reasons The Church of Jesus Christ of Latter-day Saints (the Mormons) continues to deny complicity in the Mountain Meadows Massacre — although an abundance of evidence makes clear that they led it — is because there are in Arkansas and elsewhere descendants of the 121 people killed on that September day in 1857. Many of those descendants might not be averse to suing this now very prosperous church.

I have visited all but one of these famous massacre sites — the Sacramento River Massacre of 1846 is so forgotten that its site near the northern California village of Vina can only be approximated. It is no surprise to report that none of the sites are exactly pleasant places to be, though the Camp Grant site north of Tucson does have a pretty community college nearby. In general, the taint that followed the terror still lingers, and is still powerful enough to affect locals who happen to live in the area. None of the massacres was effectively covered up, though the Sacramento River Massacre was overlooked for a very long time.

But the lesson, if it is a lesson, is that blood — in time, and, often, not that much time — will out. In case after case the dead have managed to assert a surprising potency.

In 1886 the historian and journalist J. P. Dunn published a pioneering study of Western massacres. He called his book *Massacres of the Mountains*, though few of the massacres he described actually took place in mountainous country; none of those that I am concerned with do.

The 1864 massacre at Sand Creek, in eastern Colorado, occurred in vast and still almost empty plains country. Dunn's book was a very popular account of the long and bloody war between whites and Indians (and, occasionally, Hispanics) during the long struggle for control of our Western lands. Dunn's title was catchy and his material vivid, to say the least.

Though overwritten and overlong, Dunn's book is a Black Book, of a sort that was only to become common after World War I. He had initially intended to stop his

15

story in 1875, just before the Custer battle, but found that he could not resist following the Apache campaigns in the Southwest, which were still proceeding.

Nor, in the end, could he resist doing the Little Bighorn and the subsequent troubles with the Nez Percé and the Utes. Geronimo and his eighteen warriors didn't surrender to General Nelson Miles until 1886, the year Dunn's book was published.

The Ghost Dance troubles among the Dakota Sioux, Sitting Bull's controversial death, and the final tragic slaughter at Wounded Knee Creek were still four years ahead. After 1890 there continued to be plenty of white-Indian conflict — *The New York Times* as recently as October 29, 2002, reported that there was yet again trouble at the Pine Ridge Agency in South Dakota, not far from where the Wounded Knee Massacre took place. Plenty of troubles there have been, but no more massacres on the one-hundred-victim scale.

Massacres of the Mountains is still in print; it remains interesting today not merely for what J. P. Dunn reported — often in prose more than a little purple-tinted, as we shall see — but also for what he himself *felt* about these bloody troubles. He knew well, and repeats over and over

16

again, that the Indians were commonly the victims of massive and cruel injustices — systematic injustices at that. He knew and insists that the agency system, which put the Indians on the public dole, was, time and time again, used as a personal piggy bank by corrupt administrators. The Great Sioux Uprising in Minnesota in 1862 would not have occurred had the agents just given the starving Indians the food that was both available and theirs by right.

J. P. Dunn knew that many of the Indian grievances were just ones. By the time he wrote his book it was clear that the Indians were beaten — which is not to say that they were pacified. The personal element that lends his graphic text its tension is that J. P. Dunn was close enough to the frontier experience to have felt, himself, some of the apprehension about Indian attack that was, from the early seventeenth century until almost the end of the nineteenth, a constant presence for pioneers as they strove to expand the Western frontier.

Similarly, apprehension about what the well-armed whites might do was something Indians in the line of advance seldom felt free to ignore.

This deep, constant *apprehension,* which neither the pioneers nor the Indians escaped, has, it seems to me, been too seldom factored in by historians of the settlement era, though certainly it saturates the diary literature of the pioneers, particularly the diary literature produced by frontier women, who were, of course, the likeliest candidates for rapine and kidnapping.

In my opinion this grinding, long-sustained apprehension played its part in the ultimate resort to massacre. President George W. Bush has recently revived the doctrine of the preemptive strike, a doctrine far from new in military or quasi-military practice. Most of the massacres I want to consider were thought by their perpetrators to be preemptive strikes, justified by the claim that the attacks were punishment for past harassments by the native tribes.

It is as well to say at the outset of this inquiry that all the massacres I want to write about are subjects of controversy; in most cases the only undisputed fact about a given massacre is the date on which it occurred — almost everything else remains arguable, including body counts. What I have to say, after having spent some months with the books about these bloody events, is often opinion, conjecture, or surmise — or just a best guess.

THE
VULNERABLE PIONEER

My own grandparents were vulnerable pioneers, which is perhaps one reason I began this inquiry. They left violence-torn western Missouri in the 1870s, looking for a safer place in which to raise a family. In their first travels westward I suspect they felt the apprehension regarding Indian attack that I mentioned in the previous chapter. The power of the Comanches and the Kiowa had been broken by 1875; and yet my grandparents, like many pioneers, must have wondered in their first Texas years if these formidable people were really going to *stay* broken.

As luck would have it they found in Archer County a nice piece of prairie with a good flowing spring on it, and they settled — the family seat, as it happened, was only a few miles from where one of the last small massacres on the southern plains had taken place. This was the Warren Wagon

Train Raid, in which some Kiowa, including two famous chiefs, Satank and Satanta, had drifted well south of their reservation — they fell on a luckless little convoy of teamsters hauling goods between two forts. A few teamsters escaped but seven were caught, hacked up, and burned in the traditional way. General William Tecumseh Sherman was in the area, on an inspection tour of some of the Texas forts, but the Kiowa managed to miss Sherman, who, in any case, was traveling with a well-armed escort.

General Sherman had the good luck to be "missed" more than once by formidable Indians. In 1877, while visiting Yellowstone, he narrowly avoided riding into the path of the fleeing Nez Percé, who were mopping up on all and sundry as they made their dramatic dash for Canada.

Sherman, while at Fort Richardson, near the town of Jacksboro, heard about the attack and at once instigated a pursuit that in time resulted in the arrest of the principal participants.

My grandparents' homeplace was only about a dozen miles from the site of this massacre: they can scarcely have failed to have felt some apprehension. Even fifteen years after the event it was still possible for renegade Indians to drift off the Oklahoma reservations; some probably wouldn't have sniffed at the chance to chop up a few of the settlers, who had, after all, taken their country. Small attacks *did* occur all over the West in the transition period between 1875 and the turn of the century. Had a few last diehards decided to drift south from Fort Sill my grandparents would have been their natural prey. Fear of attack was a worry shared by virtually every frontier family, and it was a worry slow to fade.

Complete safety has probably always been chimerical everywhere. As I was driving up the Nebraska-Colorado border, after visiting Sand Creek, three would-be bank robbers, on the other side of Nebraska, stormed into a bank in the small town of Norfolk just as the bank opened — probably before the cashiers had even gotten the money in their drawers. Perhaps the would-be robbers, who were Hispanic, didn't realize that in a small plains town it's apt to take an hour or so for the banks to get up-to-speed. These three men were only in the bank forty seconds, but that was time enough to kill five people stone dead. They effected a kind of small massacre of the sort that occurs frequently in America. At the same time, far to the east, two snipers were

21

terrorizing the D.C. suburbs: they killed ten people and wounded three, a kind of mini-massacre of randomly chosen victims.

Just as arbitrarily, a few years back, a loner named George Hennard strolled into a packed cafeteria in Killeen, Texas, and quickly blew away twenty-four diners — a reminder, as was what happened on 9/11, 2001, that though we are no longer pioneers we're always vulnerable.

Still, while the arrival of homicidal violence may be impossible to predict, the ways in which it arrives differ from place to place and century to century. Fifty to one hundred (or more) armed men are not now likely to race onto an Indian reservation and shoot or hack down anyone and anything they see (for raiders sometimes killed Indian horses too). These sorts of doings were chapters in the long and successful effort at dispossession that went on in the American West through the second half of the nineteenth century.

Near the end of his life the tenacious Sioux chief Red Cloud remarked that while the whites had made his people many promises, more than he could remember, they had only kept one: "They said they would take our land and they took it."

The bloody work that taking it required is the subject of this book.

THE BIG MASSACRES
AND SOME OTHERS

The massacres I want to look at closely in this inquiry are six:

The Sacramento River Massacre:
Spring 1846
The Mountain Meadows Massacre:
September 11, 1857
The Sand Creek Massacre:
November 29, 1864
The Marias River Massacre:
January 23, 1870
The Camp Grant Massacre:
April 30, 1871
The Wounded Knee Massacre:
December 29, 1890

In addition I want to consider two well-known and much studied military massacres, Fetterman and Custer, where something occurred that is rather rare in military history: the total wipeout, a battle in which one side succeeds in annihilating the other to the last man. This happened at Fort Phil Kearny in 1866 and at the Little Bighorn a decade later. (It also happened at the Alamo, which is outside my scope.)

These six massacres were dreadful events, leaving scar tissue that will always be a part of our history. But they were not without precedent. Patricia Nelson Limerick and others have reminded us forcefully that massacres of Indians did not start in the West. The whole continent was strongly contested: the Indians yielded up none of it easily. But, first or last, East or West, the Indians were up against people with better equipment; as the whites continued to push westward, many massacres, large and small, occurred. The elimination of some seven hundred Pequots, many of them burned alive in a stockade, is one of the most frequently mentioned Eastern massacres.

Some years ago I wrote a screenplay about one interesting frontier encounter, a small massacre that occurred in what is now Indiana, in 1824. I was adapting a novel based on this massacre, Jessamyn West's *The Massacre at Fall Creek*; my adaption has yet to reach the screen, though it still might.

In the Fall Creek incident, records of which are scanty indeed, settlers on what was then the very edge of the advancing frontier made a preemptive strike against a small band of Indians who were foraging, fishing, picking berries. Nine Indians were killed in the attack — most of the bodies were thrown down a well. Like many such attackers, the settlers near Fall Creek considered that they had merely been taking protective measures; in this case, though, instead of reducing the threat to their families, they increased it. The powerful tribes to the north and to the west were outraged — suddenly the whole frontier came under threat. The Indians were thought to be planning a massive, coordinated attack.

Up to this point in time, according to Jessamyn West, it had not, as a matter of law, been a crime to kill Indians; but the government, headed by President James Monroe, became fearful of a widespread revolt. The hastily arrived at solution to the crisis was to make Indian-killing a crime retroactively. A show trial was rapidly convened: able attorneys were provided both for the prosecution and the defense. The Indians, in all their power and majesty, came to witness this strange instance of white man's justice. In the end three white men were hanged by their own neighbors; one boy was spared. The Indians stayed off the warpath for a time, though plenty of war was to follow.

The massacre at Fall Creek was a very obscure incident — how much of what Jessamyn West wrote was based on historical research and how much on her imagination is now difficult to say.

To me the most interesting aspect is that (if this hastily created "law" was actually put in place) it didn't work. Many more Indians were killed, by many more whites; it was to be a good long time in America before white men were judicially punished for killing Indians.

THE
MORAL TAINT

It is clear from the records that moral op-
probrium did in time attach itself to many
of the men who planned and executed the
murders described in this book; but, in
most cases, that was as far as matters went.
The exception to this is John Doyle Lee,
who — twenty years after the killing — was
offered up by the Mormon church and
made to take the blame for the Mountain
Meadows Massacre. He was justly outraged
at this turn of events, but the higher-ups in
the Mormon church had decided to give
the public a sacrifice, in the hopes that then
the whole matter would be forgotten. (They
were wrong about that; two books about
Mountain Meadows have been published
within the last year.)

John Doyle Lee, outraged or not, was
duly executed.

The sharpest contradiction to my point
about the moral taint is surely John Milton

27

Chivington, the fighting parson who organized and led the attack at Sand Creek in 1864. Chivington neither relented nor repented; he weathered the controversy with his head unbowed. Though he resigned from the army, he was never charged or punished. There were critics, but, in general, Chivington remained a hero to his fellow Coloradans — to many he is a hero to this day. There is even a town named for him in southeastern Colorado, only a few miles from the massacre site — Chivington, Colorado, a kind of ghost hamlet, not far north of the Arkansas River.

Be as that may, there are yet those dead human beings — young, old, and in-between — who died in the massacres. They lost their lives, but not their moral potency. Hard as the men were who carried out these slaughters, conscience did, in time, stir in many of them. Long after the bodies had become merely bones, there were men who felt compelled to describe the horror they had participated in. Blame was imperfectly assessed, but guilt and outrage did make itself felt even in these small, vulnerable frontier communities. In most cases official inquiries were held, at the end of which the massacres were condemned. General Ulysses S. Grant himself called Sand Creek "murder," and he later said the same about the killings at Camp Grant. This may not seem like much but it was important: Grant was a well-respected man. Even now inquiries are going on about the more recent massacres in Bosnia and Rwanda. *Mass murder doesn't go unnoticed!* The repugnance decent people feel when faced with the slaughter of innocents eventually finds expression, though in many cases, no doubt, the worst killers, the really evil ones, entirely escape judicial reckoning. They probably sleep soundly and die unmolested in their beds. Only occasionally is an Eichmann or a Barbie brought to the bar.

During these massacres in the American West there were those who wished, as the killing went on and the blood spurted, that they had had the good sense not to saddle up that day. A good many of these eventually expressed rather dazed regrets; they had failed to anticipate that the reduction of one hundred or more human beings to the condition of meat in a meat shop would be as terrible as it turned out to be.

These belated repentings didn't change the terrible killings, but the fact that civilized human judgment finally rejects massacre is a hopeful sign.

Did Kit
Regret?

Even the scout and Indian fighter Kit Carson, who had a strong stomach when it came to killing Indians, may have turned a little, conscience-wise, after taking part in the "perfect butchery" at the Sacramento River in 1846. This turning, if it occurred, didn't prevent him from effecting the dreadful removal of the Navaho and the Mescalero Apache from their homelands in the 1860s. Kit invariably did what his superiors told him to do, whether he liked it or not; but, in these last instances, it is clear that he *didn't* like what he had been ordered to do. He was nearing the end of his life, and, by this time, knew as much about Indians as any Westerner — more, certainly, than any of his superiors knew. It may be that he finally came to understand what a tragic undertaking these removals were — in fact they were slow massacres, people dying and dying as they struggled to keep

30

up in what the Navaho call the Long Walk.

Did Kit Carson wonder, at the end, if the whole enterprise of exploration and settlement, in which he had been perhaps the preeminent guide, or, at least, the guide who lasted the longest, had been worth it? Had it been, after all, a good thing? The right thing? What he felt we will never know. Except for a brief, dictated autobiography, Kit Carson, for forty years a scout in the dangerous West, kept his conclusions, if any, to himself.

John Chivington, long before he organized the attack at Sand Creek, had come to believe that he had an absolute right to kill Indians. He made it clear, when the time came to ride, that he didn't want to hear from anyone who harbored sympathy for the Cheyenne and the Arapaho. Reportedly he even told one volunteer that he longed to "wade in gore."

At the Sacramento River, Kit Carson actually did wade in gore — it doesn't seem that he enjoyed the experience.

John Milton Chivington never turned; he defended the action at Sand Creek to the very end of his life. Carson, who remained loyal to John Charles Frémont despite the Pathfinder's many moral lapses, expressed no fondness for Chivington. Kit Carson took part in many, many Indian fights. It's possible that, at the end, he would have welcomed peace.

A decent bibliography of the literature relating to these massacres would run to at least sixty or seventy volumes: and that would not include the hundreds of books that deal with Custer and the Little Bighorn. And yet it was Kit Carson — an illiterate scout — who produced the best phrase about the business of massacre when he referred to "a perfect butchery."

All these massacres produced abundant butchery, fits of violence so extreme that they quite drove out reason. The few survivors and the many perpetrators alike were stunned by what had occurred. They were stunned to such a degree that it makes it difficult to judge the reliability of their comments, some of which were not delivered until months or years after the event. Some refused to speak of the massacre at all, while others, Ancient Mariner–like, seemed compelled to reveal the worst, and reveal it over and over again. Others made stumbling, rambling efforts to make it all seem less bad than it had been.

Only the hardest cases, the true believers,

display absolute conviction. Those less firm often try to construct self-exculpatory defenses. It is not always easy for the chronicler to decide what testimony, if any, can be relied upon, though, in my opinion, people who lie about the massacres have a value to the record too. The lies people make up about extreme actions may be as revelatory as the few truths they manage to cough up.

After several of these massacres, even the most hardened of the perpetrators gave vent to wild exaggerations, particularly where body counts were concerned. Chivington, after Sand Creek, at first reported that he had killed between five and six hundred Indians, or rather more than had been in the camp to begin with — the actual figure was around 140, the same number the historian Sally Denton gives for the Mountain Meadows dead, and very close to the count at Wounded Knee (146).

The most difficult thing for the historian of these massacres to judge is tone of voice. We may know what someone said, but how did he or she say it? Take Kit Carson's "perfect butchery" remark. He said it, but in what tone: happily, matter-of-factly, wearily, with an element of sadness or disgust in his tone? Did he sound resigned? Kit Carson had seen much Western death. He had killed Indians and scalped them, but most of his battles had been small-scale endeavors, a few Indians versus a few mountain men; they were bloody fights, to be sure, but still on a very different scale from what happened on the Sacramento River.

Chivington's tone we may guess at; he was almost always angry, even when he was not killing Indians. But what about Brigham Young's tone, or tones, during the years when he was trying to cover up Mountain Meadows? At the time the massacre occurred the U.S. Army was on its way to Utah, to curb Mormon excesses. As it happened, the army didn't get there until the following year, but at this juncture Brigham Young would have been careful not to say anything too inflammatory. But he was thunderous and fiery when he demanded that the Mormons of southern Utah hew to the official line, which was that the Paiute Indians did the killing. Brigham Young was a politician as well as a church leader; he had more than one oratorical instrument in his orchestra and he shifted skillfully from one to another. Today we'd see him on television and be able to judge for ourselves, but as it is we have to base our judgment on letters, diary entries, speeches, sermons, depositions, and records whose provenance is not always well established.

In the case of most of these massacres, the tones in the reports seem to vary between jeremiad and lament — battle reports through the ages often do much the same. Few observers of what happened at Sand Creek or Wounded Knee were impartial. The participants in the massacres were either trying to kill people, or trying to avoid being killed by people, a circumstance that doesn't enhance one's objectivity.

Everyone who has written about these massacres admits at some point that they are required to make judgments on the basis of very quivery evidence. The ground is rarely firm or the truth plain.

Nothing illustrates this better than the vexed question of body counts, which is where I'd like to begin my inquiry.

COUNTS

The very first thing one notices when sifting through these reports of massacres — whether personal, official, or journalistic — is that the body counts vary widely from report to report. As good an example as any are the body counts from Wounded Knee.

When I first began to rummage around in this literature I went first to *The New Encyclopedia of the American West*, published by Yale, an invaluable reference book that I use virtually every day. I looked up Wounded Knee first, where I found what I already knew: that the reason the U.S. Army decided, on that fateful day in 1890, to arrest Chief Big Foot and remove his people to a different, distant agency was part of a broad effort to suppress the Ghost Dance, a recently arrived religious phenomenon that — puzzlingly in my view — made both the military and civil authorities in South Dakota extremely nervous. (I will return to the matter of official anxiety before we are done.)

Before reading the whole of the long Wounded Knee entry, I flipped back to the Ghost Dance entry, where I read that "almost three hundred Indian men, women, and children were massacred by the 7th Cavalry."

That figure was higher than any I had previously seen for this massacre; other sources had put the dead at between two hundred and 230.

But when I flipped back again in my big reference book to the entry on Wounded Knee and read on through the article, the figure given there was 146 Indian dead; 146 also happens to be the figure given on the big historical marker at the site itself.

Time, and patient counting, had whittled down the figure given in the Ghost Dance entry by more than half.

It is well to remember that the Sioux, at Wounded Knee, though surprised and vastly outgunned, still managed to account for a good many soldiers, perhaps as many as thirty-one.

The widest and wildest swings in numbers of estimated dead at the other massacres are to be found in the histories of Sand Creek. Chivington's estimate of five to six hundred is the high figure, and seventy is the low figure. The number of troopers killed is usually put at fourteen, some of whom died off site.

Present-day thinking about Sand Creek, as I have said, is that about 140 Indians died. Only seven prisoners were taken, two women and five children, all of whom were soon left at nearby Fort Lyon.

Lieutenant James Bradley made the first body count of army dead after the Battle of the Little Bighorn, in 1876. At the battlefield itself he counted 197 bodies — probably a pretty accurate figure just for the men of Custer's command, though it left out Major Reno's casualty figures, which Lieutenant Bradley was still unaware of. Major Reno lost thirty-two men, with 152 wounded. How many of the wounded later died I don't know.

The Battle of the Little Bighorn was one of the most famous battles ever fought on American soil. There were soon to be recounts and recounts; in a sense the process continues to this day.

What of the Indian losses in that battle? First reports suggested two hundred Indians died, but, over time, this count has been whittled way down. More recent estimates put the number of Indian dead at forty-five. If you add to that the thirty-six warriors that Crazy Horse claimed had been killed at the Battle of the Rosebud, one week earlier, you get some eighty dead Indians, an enormous loss for a hunter-gatherer society; but, of course, these dead died in glorious triumphs — the numbers of the fallen did not dilute the triumph much.

It is well to remember that Fetterman, the Rosebud, and the Little Bighorn were the greatest victories the Plains Indians ever achieved.

Of these, of course, the Battle of the Little Bighorn was the greatest. It was also the last.

It should be remembered too that Fetterman, the Rosebud, and the Little Bighorn were *battles,* warrior against warrior, which sets them off from the massacres I'm considering here. In these massacres many more women and children were killed than fighting men.

At the Camp Grant Massacre, for example, except for one old man and a "well-grown boy," *no* warriors were killed, only women and children. Throughout the era of the massacres it was, overwhelmingly, women and children who were massacred.

In the Sacramento River Massacre, Kit Carson said frankly that he had no idea how many were killed, but two other participants in that slaughter tried to guess at the number. Thomas Martin thought the dead numbered between 175 and 250, whereas Thomas Breckenridge thought the dead numbered between 120 and 150.

Our confidence in these counts must be tempered somewhat by the wildly varying guesses these same three men made as to how many Indians were there in the first place. Thomas Martin thought there were between four and five *thousand,* Kit Carson estimated one thousand, and Thomas Breckenridge, whose guess was probably the most accurate, thought there might have been around four hundred, of which perhaps 150 were warriors and the rest women and children.

When one is heading into mortal, no-quarter-given combat, careful counting is the last thing most people would attempt. A more or less normal fear instinct would encourage participants to think they see more Indians than are actually there.

The frequent variation in post-massacre body counts is also explainable. Having just participated in the killing of more than one hundred human beings in an irrational spasm of violence, one would not be likely, while the blood of the living is cooling and the blood of the victims still soaking into the ground, to be able to wander through the meat shop and produce an accurate count.

In the Custer battle, incidentally, there was a good deal of decapitation as well as more routine mutilations. Quite a few limbs were also chopped off — it would not be hard, in such a context, for a counter such as Lieutenant James Bradley to overlook a corpse or two.

Massacres may be many things, but they are never neat — they might be considered the very antithesis of neatness. Not everyone died in a nice countable line; in fact, almost no one did. Some fled, some were chased; many were wounded, often mortally. Many of these last died at some distance from the center of the fight. A few might crawl away and live for days before dying. At Wounded Knee four Sioux babies and one or two women were found alive some days after the massacre, although a blizzard had passed through in the meantime. The resilience of babies, particularly, has been noticed in many such contexts.

It could be too that there are basic psychological reasons why body counts vary so greatly. Counting is a rational activity, requiring at least a little brainpower, whereas slaughtering people is a process during which reason is best negated. In indiscriminate killing reason gets pushed aside: the two modes, slaughtering and counting, are opposed. No one was carving notches while the bullets flew at Sand Creek or Wounded Knee.

Though body counts still meant something in the Vietnam War, most modern military conflicts have spread death on such a vast scale as to render counting irrelevant, and also impossible. In the firebombing of the German cities in World War II the intense heat of the fires left nothing countable, just globules of fat. How many *did* die in Dresden or Hiroshima? The count can only be approximate, as on a smaller scale, it still is for the victims of 9/11.

The massacres of the American West were intimate affairs compared to the vast impersonal slaughters that modern weaponry makes possible now.

The vocabulary of atrocity has always been rather limited. There are at most a couple of dozen ways in which deadly violence can be visited quickly on a human body, even a human community: these few are repeated endlessly, almost inescapably in every massacre. You can burn a body, hack it up, decapitate it, cut off — or out — its genitalia, smash its skull, tear fetuses out of pregnant women, shoot arrows or bullets into it, maybe rip out its heart or other organs; and, really, that is more or less the whole menu.

Usually most of the above can be accomplished by expert warriors in a very short time, as was proven at the Fetterman Massacre when eighty men were killed and thoroughly mutilated in only about half an hour.

What remained on that field was a meat shop, a deathscape out of Brueghel.

At the Little Bighorn the women of the Sioux and Cheyenne walked amid the pale white corpses and added a touch or two of their own — puncturing Custer's eardrums with awls, for example. He was not otherwise mutilated, but the women of the Sioux and Cheyenne did not want Long Hair (Custer) arriving in the spirit world fully intact.

In the grisly massacre at Sand Creek, where a battle of sorts raged for hours, scope was found for some inventiveness on the part of Chivington's more hardened Indian-haters. One hundred scalps were collected later to be exhibited in a Denver theater. The audience cheered wildly, and might have cheered even more wildly had there been two hundred scalps. At Sand Creek, mutilation of the dead was so common that it is commented on in virtually every account. Scrotums became tobacco pouches; the pudenda of the women were removed and used as hatbands or saddle horn covers.

And yet there does seem to be a human hunger for accuracy when it comes to keeping count of the dead. In almost all massacres there are, at first, conflicting sets of figures, a high and a low. Almost always patient investigation revises the figure downward: from six hundred to 140 at Sand Creek, from three hundred to 146 at Wounded Knee. People confronted with massacres at first want to know how many died — a little later some of them begin to want to know why.

IMAGES,

HEROES, STARS

When Paul Andrew Hutton produced his *Custer Reader* in 1992, he estimated that there existed at least 967 graphic representations — paintings, prints, drawings, sketches in newspapers — of Custer's Last Stand.

The two most famous representations of this event are paintings: John Mulvany's *Custer's Last Rally*, and Cassilly Adams's *Custer's Last Fight*. The latter, updated a bit by Otto Becker and published in a wide variety of formats — trays, calendars, handouts — by the Anheuser-Busch Company of St. Louis, was probably the one picture most Americans had seen. A copy of it hung in the barbershop in Archer City in my youth.

Custer's Last Fight, as Paul Andrew Hutton points out, is a wholly imaginary rendering of the famous encounter at the Little Bighorn. No white witness survived

45

the battle. Many Indians — thousands — did survive it, and quite a few of them later had something to say about the deaths of Long Hair and his men; but it seems highly unlikely that either Mulvany or Adams attempted to reconcile their personal visions with those of actual witnesses to the battle.

Besides — as I point out in my short biography of Crazy Horse — the dust that would have been thrown up by those thousands of charging horses would have made any synoptic look at the battle quite impossible. Dust and horses and a glimpse now and then of a charging warrior or a weary doomed soldier are about as much as anyone could have seen.

Unquestionably, though, the two paintings helped shape a national myth, more or less as the many cheap pictures of Roland holding off the Saracens at the pass of Roncevaux have become part of the French national myth.

For Custer the stream of images continues to flow. Leonard Baskin's somber frontispiece to Evan Connell's *Son of the Morning Star* is a notable example — it catches something of the darkness that was in the man. Many films have featured Custer, one of the most notable being

Arthur Penn's fine adaptation of Thomas Berger's *Little Big Man.*

Americans' lack of passion for history is well known. History may not quite be bunk, as Henry Ford suggested, but there's no denying that, as a people, we sustain a passionate concentration on the present and the future.

Backward is just not a natural direction for Americans to look — historical ignorance remains a national characteristic. When it comes to the Old West, subject of thousands of books and almost as many thousands of movies, most Americans now know only the broadest generalizations. They know that the settling of the West involved crossing vast plains and high mountains, sometimes in covered wagons. Most know that there was a gold rush or two; most know, also, that there were Indians there before us, most of whom did not want us taking their land — or land that they considered to be theirs. We, of course, considered that it ought to be ours, so we took it. There were many battles, and the Indians were defeated.

Now there are excellent histories covering almost every aspect of our successful conquest of the West — a complex often confusing process — but not many Americans read them. Their knowledge of the winning of the West is mostly arrived at iconographically, from movies, and the movie images possess enormous power. Regarded collectively, movie Westerns have done more to determine our idea of the West than all the books ever written about it, good or bad. If Custer's Last Stand could only have taken place in Monument Valley, the single most powerful landscape could have framed the single most powerful story; and that, so far as most people were concerned, would be quite enough to know about the Old West, thank you.

The movies, by their nature, favor only a few stars, and only a few real national heroes. Of the thousands of interesting characters who played a part in winning the West, only a bare handful have any real currency with the American public now. Iconographically, even Lewis and Clark haven't really survived, though Sacagawea has. With the possible exception of Kit Carson, none of the mountain men mean anything today. Kit Carson's name vaguely suggests the Old West to many people, but not one in a million of them will have any distinct idea as to what Kit did.

The roster of still-recognizable Westerners probably boils down to Custer, Buffalo Bill

Cody, Billy the Kid, and perhaps Wild Bill Hickok. Theodore Roosevelt, a Westerner manqué, would once have made the list, but not today. Custer, Cody, and Billy the Kid are clearly the top three, generating far more imagery than any of the other candidates.

Skimpy as the image bank is for white Westerners, it is even skimpier for Indians. My guess would be that only Sacagawea, Sitting Bull, and Geronimo still ring any bells with the general public. Crazy Horse, who never allowed his image to be captured, is still important to Indians as a symbol of successful resistance, but less so to whites. Even a chief such as Red Cloud, so renowned in his day that he went to New York and made a speech at Cooper Union, is now only known to historians, history buffs, and a few Nebraskans.

At the broadest level, only the white stars Custer, Cody, and Billy the Kid, and two tough Indians, Sitting Bull and Geronimo, are the people the public thinks about when it thinks about the Old West.

THE SACRAMENTO RIVER MASSACRE, SPRING 1846

If my argument in the previous chapter is valid, then it should be no surprise that today the Sacramento River Massacre is, of these six tragic events, much the least known. From what I can find, the first historian to give it more than a paragraph or two is David Roberts, in his excellent study of Kit Carson and John Charles Frémont: the book is called *A Newer World*. Carson was Frémont's principal guide on the popular explorer's first three expeditions into the American West.

In 1846, when the massacre occurred, there were no particularly famous Indians. Tecumseh, plenty famous in his day, had been dead since 1813. California produced no famous Indians, then or later, with the exception of the martyred Captain Jack of the Modocs. The battle for the Great Plains hadn't yet started: we are well in advance of Crazy Horse, Red Cloud,

Sitting Bull, and the rest.

The men who effected the massacre at the Sacramento River could probably not even have named the tribes their victims belonged to. David Roberts believes that the Indians dancing by the water were a mixture of Maidu, Wintu, and Yana, names that meant not much then and nothing now, except to very close students of Californian Indian life.

Most Indian tribes were largely unknown, except to the explorers or trappers who went among them, but, when it came to near total obscurity, the California Indians were in a class by themselves. To the whites who slaughtered them they were merely nameless savages, the quicker killed the better. When the Gold Rush started they were swept away in the thousands, with brutal efficiency.

John Charles Frémont, the Pathfinder as he was called (though he found no paths), was aware of the Paiute tribe, to the east of the Sierras, and of the Klamaths, to the north of where he was camped at that time; but it was unlikely that he had even heard the names of the tribes he allowed his men to slaughter. Maidu. Wintu? Yana? It's doubtful that these terms meant a thing to John Charles Frémont.

To this day, for that matter, the California Indians have contributed almost nothing to the popular iconography of the West. There is, as I said, the noble Captain Jack, hero and victim.

Then there was Willie Boy, a Morongo who, mad for love, kidnapped his beloved and led the posse that pursued them on an epic, almost five-hundred-mile chase across the desert. When the game was up he killed both the girl and himself — Robert Redford starred in a movie about him. Willie Boy made his run in 1909.

The movies were revving up by that time, but the movies didn't do that much with California Indian life, although both Mary Pickford and Dolores del Rio played Ramona, from Helen Hunt Jackson's novel of the same name, about a beautiful but ill-starred half-breed girl and her doomed Indian husband.

If David Roberts is right, then it's likely that a great many Maidu, Wintu, and Yana did gather on the banks of the Sacramento River in the spring of 1846, where their numbers and demeanor soon began to frighten the local whites. Possibly the Indians had merely come to the river to practice their own spring rituals.

The only force handy with sufficient strength to disperse the Indians was the group of men with Frémont, who was in California on his third exploring expedition. His first expedition, four years back, had made Frémont a national hero — he was easily America's most famous explorer, and fame had rather gone to his head.

In fact, by 1846 Frémont's principal achievements were already behind him, but neither Frémont nor anyone else suspected this at the time. Since the massacre is now mainly a footnote to Frémont's career, a word about this third expedition might be in order.

Frémont actually worked for the Army Corps of Topographical Engineers; he *was* a first-rate topographer. His orders on this occasion had been to survey rivers flowing *east* out of the Rockies, which, obviously, did not include the Sacramento, but Frémont, vain as a prince, at once delegated this tame assignment and made straight for California — he had been there once previously and suspected that the Mexican government, which was spread very thin, might soon collapse. If he could only manage to be in the right place at the right time, California — a major plum —

might drop in his lap, in which case even more glory would be his. So he wandered up and down the state, more or less passively; when something *did* happen in the north — the Bear Flag Revolt — he postured a good deal but offered no real help.

Just before he headed north to the Sacramento River he decided, rather cavalierly, to challenge the Mexican authorities in Monterey. He and his men occupied a nearby hill — Gavilan Peak — threw up some breastworks, raised the American flag, and waited for the Mexicans to attack, which they declined to do. The flag fluttered in the breeze for three days; then the breeze became a gale and the flag blew down. The Pathfinder decided that honor had been satisfied, so he packed up his troop and went north. This strange retreat earned Frémont the undying contempt of the famous rather dandified mountain man Joseph Walker, who said Frémont was the worst coward, morally and physically, that he had ever known.

Frémont didn't know it, but his adventure in California was to end even less gloriously because of his refusal to recognize the authority of General Stephen Watts Kearny, who, after the Mexican defeat, took the Pathfinder back to Washington and court-martialed him.

Meanwhile, though, Frémont took his men far to the north, past Sutter's Fort, to bivouac for a time at the ranch of Peter Lassen, where the Sacramento River comes out of the mountains. Not long after Frémont's arrival, the Indians also arrived and the locals began to get nervous. They asked Frémont for protection. What happened next is related by Thomas Martin, in a memoir that surfaced in 1878:

They asked Fremont to protect them. He replied that he had no right to fight Indians but he told us that those who wished to take part in the expedition against the Indians he would discharge and take us again afterward. . . . At the foot of the low hills where the Sacramento River comes out of the mountains . . . we found the Indians to the number of 4,000 to 5,000 on a tongue of land between the bends of the river, having a war dance preparatory to attacking the settlers. Our advance guard of 36 immediately charged and poured a volley into them killing 24. They then rushed them with sabres. The rest of the party came up and charged in among them and in less than 3 hours we had killed

175 of them. Most of the Indians escaped into the neighboring mountains.

His fellow writer Thomas Breckenridge, however, thought the war party, if it *was* a war party, consisted of "only 150 bucks and 250 women and children."
Kit Carson's brief commentary agreed with neither of the above as to the number of Indians awaiting them:

> During our stay at Lawson's [Lassen's] some Americans that were settled in the neighborhood came in stating that there were about 1,000 Indians in the vicinity making preparations to attack the settlements: requested assistance of Fremont to drive them back. He and party and some Americans that lived near started for the Indians encampment, found them in great numbers, and war started.

"He and party" seems to have convinced various biographers that Frémont led the attack, an action that would have been, for John Charles Frémont, entirely out of character. Unlike Chivington, Frémont had no desire at all to wade in gore. He rarely (if ever) fought, preferring, as his biographer Andrew Rolle observed, to use Kit Carson as a hit man. Kit was a thorough hit man too.

Thomas Martin's account, if examined closely, seems rather startling. If the advance guard of thirty-six men thought there were four to five thousand waiting for them, then they were certainly bold to launch an attack: as bold as Custer was, thirty years later.

Even if the first volley killed twenty-four, that still left a lot of Indians; many would have thought twice before attacking this group with sabers. Even if we lower the count to Breckenridge's four hundred, a saber attack was still bold. And if twenty-four fell to a single volley, why would it take three hours to kill 175? Is it not rather odd that Thomas Martin could count the victims of the first volley when thousands of Indians were still ranged against them? A mere twenty-four killed would not have made much of a dent.

Of course if Breckenridge was right and there were only four hundred Indians there, twenty-four would have made a significant dent.

That the men immediately waded in with sabers seems odd too. If the first volley was so effective, why not keep shooting? Hand-to-hand combat would have seemed far more dangerous. Were the attackers in the grip of such a blood frenzy that they couldn't stop, producing the "perfect butchery" that Kit Carson talks about?

The aloof John Charles Frémont, once the operation was seen to be a success, as usual makes it appear that he had been the prime mover, while getting no actual blood on his hands. The lesson administered, he says, "was rude but necessary, and had the desired effect."

David Roberts deserves much credit for addressing the Sacramento River Massacre in *A Newer World*. His own suspicion, backed up by what anthropological studies there are, was that the Indians had gathered to celebrate a spring ritual, possibly the Bear Dance, which the whites, unfamiliar with this ritual, mistook for a war dance.

The Maidu and Wintu were fairly settled, sedentary tribes, acorn-gatherers, salmon-fishers. Their numbers shrank so precipitously during the second half of the nineteenth century that by the time the anthropologists got there there were few left to study.

The much publicized Ishi, last of the Yana tribe, *was* studied, by the anthropologist Theodora Kroeber, but she knew nothing of this massacre and did not try to determine if some trace of it survived in Yana lore or memory.

In a sense the Sacramento River Massacre illustrates a problem that was to bedevil white-Indian relations from first to last: the inability, on the part of whites, to distinguish between Indians who were friendly and Indians who were hostile. Any big gathering of Indians, however well intentioned, made whites nervous — to a degree it still does.

One of the continuing sources of disagreement about the Sand Creek Massacre is that John Chivington led his troopers into the camp of Black Kettle, probably the single best known peace Indian of that day. Black Kettle was so sure that he enjoyed protection that he desperately waved an American flag even as the Coloradans were mowing down his people.

From the first there were plenty of people in the West — indeed, in the country — who were frankly exterminationists. They wanted all the Indians gone. It may be that a disproportionate number of these genocidally minded settlers made their way to California. The deaths at the Sacramento River were merely a prelude to the rapid elimination of the California Indians.

For a good account of this grim slaughter the reader is directed to the "Far West" chapter of James Wilson's *The Earth Shall Weep.* During the conflict with the Plains Indians, there were at least a few equal fights. In California, with the exception of the Modoc War, there were *no* equal fights. Men who believed that the only good Indian was a dead Indian overwhelmingly prevailed. During the Gold Rush particularly, exterminationists were thick on the ground. Indians were killed as casually as rabbits. I have reported elsewhere about a young vigilante who came to have qualms about killing Indian children with his rifle: the big bullets tore the small bodies so! The man was soon able to square his conscience by killing only adults with his rifle; the children he dispatched with his pistol.

It is only fair to say, though, that if one puts oneself in the position of an ill-trained and perhaps scrappily equipped young soldier, the distinction between friendly Indians and hostile Indians may seldom have been easy to make — or maintain —

particularly in the frightening minutes just before a fight.

Similarly, most settlers, making their lonely way across the harsh distances of the West, might naturally have found all Indians a little frightening. By the end of the settlement period particularly, most settlers would have been well aware that the Indians had been pushed off their land. Why wouldn't they have been hostile?

Also, during the whole era of conquest and conflict, there was the constant problem of the young warriors — young men raised with a warrior ethic, in a warrior society. Raiding, for these boys, was not only a right: it was necessary training and, also, the source of self-esteem.

Many a well-planned Indian ambush was blown at the last minute by the impatient young warriors, who could not wait for the right moment to attack. The Fetterman Massacre in 1866 was one of the few ambushes in which the young warriors didn't spoil the plan.

Black Kettle himself, the most dedicated of peace Indians, had as much trouble with his young warriors as any other Indian, and he admitted it.

In the 1870s particularly, warring in the West extended over a vast border-to-border territory. In the Southwest were Cochise, Victorio, Geronimo, Quanah Parker. In the north were Sitting Bull, Crazy Horse, Red Cloud. In the vast middle were the southern Cheyenne, Arapaho, Kiowa, Comanche, Osage, Pawnee. All these tribes had constantly to watch their territory shrink: they had to watch the game on which they depended slaughtered. They were up against it and they knew it. They had no reason to hold back: they found their dignity in fighting.

To some extent, perhaps, it is human nature to think the worst about those who are not as we are. Tribalism was an instinct and an organizing principle for so long that it is planted deep in the human psyche. It can rarely be civilized out of us.

It is easy to say that the army in the West should have been more particular about which bands of natives they attacked. Right now, in Iraq, we are finding out how difficult it is to hit only the bad guys when we make war. Even the best reconnaissance has its limits. Custer had excellent reconnaissance available to him on that fatal day at the Little Bighorn. He ignored it all. If someone had pointed out to Kit Carson that these Indians dancing by the Sacramento River were only doing their spring Bear Dance would he have let them be? It seems unlikely. The men were by then in a killing mood, and they killed.

Three hours of steady killing produced a well-stocked meat shop on that tongue of land. Only after it ended and tempers cooled did some of the men realize that *this* killing left a bad taste. No doubt they were excited at first, but three hours of steady killing may well have become an unpleasant chore. Some men may have become sated — walked away with their dripping sabers. Some may finally have been repulsed.

In fairness to Frémont's men, though, they were not many, and they were a long way from home. If the threat from these Indians was exaggerated by the panicky settlers, the *general* threat from Indians was real. Frémont always maintained that the only reason he attempted the nearly disastrous winter crossing of the Sierra Nevada in 1844 was because the Indians on the east side of the mountains — the Paiutes, particularly — were nibbling away at their horses and pack animals. His fear of being set afoot and having his men picked off one by one was not unreasonable.

In fact, only a few days after the Sacramento River Massacre, while camped farther north, in Klamath country, various of the party heard, during the night, a disquieting thud. Frémont got up to investigate, but found nothing. The next morning the party discovered that the thud had been the sound an axe made when it split the skull of Basil Lajeunesse, a popular man and one of Frémont's special favorites. A punitive expedition was launched immediately. Many Klamaths were killed.

Ishi, last of the Yana, desperate, tired, and hungry, only allowed himself to be coaxed into the settlements in 1911, by which time almost all the Maidu and Wintu were gone.

We are unlikely ever to know more about the massacre at the Sacramento River than can be found in *A Newer World*, whose author acknowledges many uncertainties. A bunch of Indians, gathered for what purpose we can only guess, frightened the local whites, who called down death upon an unknown number of them. Kit Carson and some of the men may have regretted it; but they were soon back to killing Klamaths, in revenge for their young friend.

In 1862, Kit Carson, obeying the command of his superior, Major James H. Carleton, reluctantly began to drive the Mescalero Apache and then the Navaho from their homes. They were marched to a prison camp on the Bosque Redondo, in eastern New Mexico. There they died in numbers that far exceeded the death toll in any Western massacre. Their trek was called the Long Walk, the Navaho Trail of Tears. All in all such removals were more deadly than any single fight. The Indians understood fighting, but no people easily accepts exile. Combatants can sometimes reconcile, but unjust exile seems to burn forever.

Kit Carson may not have been as brilliant a pure explorer as the prodigious Jedediah Smith — one of the few explorers who sought geographical knowledge for its own sake — but, for durability, Carson had no equal. He first went to California with Ewing Young in 1828: he beavered and he guided, and he was still doing it thirty-five years later. He led Frémont on three expeditions; he led many others as well. When he was done he could justly claim to have walked the whole West. The only guide who may have been his equal was the Delaware scout Black Beaver, who guided Captain Randolph Marcy on his explorations of the Red River country.

Saddened by the brutal business with the Apache and the Navaho, Kit Carson spent his last years with his beloved wife, Josefa, "Little Josie." In photographs he always looks melancholy. Josefa died, and, not long after, Kit died, sad at the end.

THE MOUNTAIN MEADOWS MASSACRE, SEPTEMBER 11, 1857

On the very day, October 12, 2002, when I sat down to begin organizing my notes on the Mountain Meadows Massacre, there appeared in *The New York Times* a long piece by Emily Eakin about that long-ago event and the still continuing controversy it has engendered. Two new books have recently been published (Will Bagley's *Blood of the Prophets* and Sally Denton's *American Massacre*), and a third — which I understand will constitute a Mormon rebuttal — is now in the press.

Scarcely two weeks later the *New York Review of Books* carried a thoughtful essay by Caroline Fraser about this same, much studied massacre. The Mormon historians who are doing the rebuttal will argue, yet again, that Brigham Young, the Mormon leader, did not order this massacre.

Mountain Meadows was again very much in the news, reinforcing my point that massacres, once exposed, just won't go away. Of the six massacres I propose to study, Mountain Meadows is much the most complicated, and it is the only one in which there may have been a theocratic motive. Things just keep coming to light — 2,605 bones and bone fragments accidentally uncovered at the monument site in 1999, for example — suggesting that we are probably still a long way from having heard the last word about Mountain Meadows.

The cornerstone of Mountain Meadows studies is Juanita Brooks's classic — and, considering that she is a devout Mormon, heroic — book, *The Mountain Meadows Massacre*, first published by Stanford in 1950 and kept in print now by the University of Oklahoma. There is a lengthy shelf of related studies, some of them by Juanita Brooks herself — the most substantial of these are listed in my bibliography.

All these books attempt to describe what happened on that dreadful September day in 1857, when a large wagon train on its way from Arkansas to California was massacred by a force composed of local Mormons and Paiute Indians. (Even here body counts differ: I thought 121 people were killed, but Sally Denton puts the count at 140.)

These various studies also attempt to determine *why* the massacre happened, and — biggest and most intractable question — who, if anyone, in the Mormon hierarchy ordered the killing. For nearly 150 years the finger of inquiry has been pointed at Brigham Young; it's an issue still very much in debate.

The final, comprehensive truth about Mountain Meadows may have remained elusive, but in fact we do know a great deal about this massacre, and evidence such as the 2,605 bone fragments just keeps appearing. (A lead scroll purporting to be John Doyle Lee's confession turned up as recently as 2002, but its authenticity seems questionable.) Talk about a massacre that won't go away.

The Church of Jesus Christ of Latter-Day Saints (the Mormons) has hoped from the first day to the present that if they just stuck together, hunkered down, and kept quiet, time would pass and people would forget.

Time did pass, but people have not even begun to forget.

When in 1999 the president of the Mormon Church, Gordon B. Hinckley, journeyed to southern Utah to dedicate the most recent of the various unsatisfactory monuments at the Mountain Meadows site, he not only declared that the truth about Mountain Meadows could never be known, but he also read a disclaimer from the church's legal team which affirmed that nothing said at the memorial service in any way implied Mormon complicity in these long-ago murders. (In less guarded moments President Hinckley has said that he suspected the local people did it.)

In suggesting that Mountain Meadows is an impenetrable mystery, President Hinckley has swung well wide of the truth. Juanita Brooks, a devout Mormon and fine historian, clearly and professionally penetrated many of these mysteries more than half a century ago, in *The Mountain Meadows Massacre*, a model of clarity. Will Bagley, Sally Denton, William Wise, and others have extended the valuable inquiry that she began.

Mountain Meadows would make a good opera. It is an American tragedy of blood. Billy the Kid's story has yielded a ballet; perhaps someday something operatic will emerge from this tragic story.

The uniqueness of Mountain Meadows for this study is that on this then grassy plain whites killed whites — or, to be more precise, whites with the help of Indians killed whites. Both Mormons and Paiutes have downplayed their part in the killing. It had long been supposed that the whites killed mostly men, and the Paiutes mainly women and children, but the bones in the mass grave uncovered in 1999 have complicated this picture — of which more later.

The immigrant train in question, the so-called Fancher party, was well armed and well equipped. There were some thirty wagons and they had made it all the way from Arkansas through dangerous territory. It is unlikely that the Paiutes alone could have overrun them. The Paiutes might have nibbled at them, as they nibbled at Frémont, but they were not temperamentally inclined to long sieges or lengthy battles.

Everyone who has written about Mountain Meadows has been at pains to point out that the massacre occurred at a moment of high tension in the Mormon capital of Salt Lake City. The tension was due to the fact that the United States Army was on its way to Utah, to address many reports of Mormon excesses. The U.S. government meant to subdue this unruly province once and for all. They also meant to replace

Brigham Young, a full-fledged theocrat, with a civil governor. At that time Brigham Young was governor of Utah *and* the head of the Mormon church. President James Buchanan was fed up, both with the Mormons in general and Brigham Young in particular. He sent the army to forcefully put matters right.

Thus, in the summer of 1857, Brigham Young and Mormons throughout Utah were gearing up to defy both the president and the army. The Mormons had been pushed steadily westward, from New York state to Illinois, Missouri, and now Utah; they didn't intend to be pushed any farther, and they didn't want to be told how they might order their theocracy. They were no strangers to mob violence. Though forbidden by their creed to shed innocent blood — a moral prohibition that was to have large consequences later — they did subscribe to a doctrine of blood atonement, which instructed them to shed the blood of gentiles — that is, non-Mormons. The Fancher party consisted entirely of gentiles, and had, moreover, the added stigma of having come from Arkansas, where, very recently, the popular Mormon prophet Parley Pratt had been murdered.

The Fancher party was already on the

road when Parley Pratt was killed — by an outraged husband whose wife the prophet coveted for his own purposes. This woman, Eleanor McComb McLean Pratt, though in appearance an unlikely Helen of Troy, was soon recovered sufficiently from her grief to proclaim the evil of gentiles and appeal for vengeance. The Fancher party, though innocent, became the prime candidate for the enactment of the doctrine of blood atonement.

Thus there were two stressful elements in the Mormon communities in the late summer of 1857: the approach of the army and the outrage over the death of Prophet Parley. The Fancher party well knew that they were not popular. Though well financed, they were often refused supplies, and those they did manage to purchase were priced to the skies. Since it was a large party, with a herd of cattle numbering between six hundred and one thousand head; and since the country ahead was desert, both supplies and forage were important. When they got to Mountain Meadows it was the abundant forage that prompted them to stop. Mountain Meadows is no longer grassy, but in 1857 it was abundantly grassed, and the party paused — as any herdsmen would — to allow the cattle to graze their fill before starting into more difficult country. Though they were close to being out of Utah, stopping was an eminently practical move for any group with hundreds of livestock to maintain.

The Paiutes and other desert Indians, who were subsisting on very little, not unnaturally wanted those cattle. A number of Mormon farmers and ranchers wanted them too. (These cattle were said to be longhorns, a breed not previously seen in Utah but abundantly available to the Arkansas party from the thousands that ran loose in nearby Texas at the time.)

Though the approach of the army was widely known and much talked about, the army, as it turned out, was having supply problems of its own. The command unit that was to march on Salt Lake City was still in far-off Laramie; the unit was not yet equipped to make the long journey across the plains with fall upon them — on those particular plains, especially what's called the Bridger Plateau, fall can be hard to tell from winter. Both can produce bitter cold.

By the time the Fancher party was attacked, on September 11 — a date that might be said to favor massacres — Brigham Young had learned that he had

74

nothing to fear from the U.S. Army that year. The supply problem was so severe that no troops would reach Salt Lake City in 1857. The big fight, if there was to be one, would not occur until the spring of the following year.

In fact, the Mormons never had to fight the army: the differences of opinion between the U.S. government and the Mormon authorities were mostly worked out in negotiations. The army did come on to Utah in 1858, but the Utah War, so called, was a big fizzle, an outcome only known long after the Fancher party had been reduced to the condition of a meat shop.

It was, though, the immigrants' misfortune to arrive in wild, lawless southwestern Utah just at a time when the Mormons were most highly stressed. It was only a day or two before the massacre that Brigham Young realized he would not soon be under attack.

Despite this element of relief, the Mormons remained stirred up. Even so, the Fancher party, had it just kept moving, might have passed through Mormon territory unmolested and gone on to the promised land of California, but for the temptation of that tall, waving grass. By stopping to let their cattle graze they made themselves an irresistible target, both to Indians and Mormons.

Six days after the massacre Brigham Young penned an entry in his diary about the likely behavior of the Indians:

A spirit seems to be taking possession of the Indians to assist Israel [the Mormons]. I can hardly restrain them from exterminating the Americans.

In fact, he didn't restrain them, and yet the very day before the massacre Young claimed to have dispatched a letter by fast courier to Elder Isaac Haight, the leader of the southern Mormons. The letter read in part:

We do not expect that any part of the Army will be able to reach here this fall . . . they are now at or near Laramie. . . . So you see that the Lord has answered our prayers, and again thwarted the blow which was aimed at our heads. In regard to the emigration trains passing through our settlements, we must not interfere with them *until they are first notified to keep away.* You must not meddle with them. The Indians we expect will do as they please, but you should try and preserve good feelings with them. There are no other trains going through that I know of. If those who are there will leave, let them go in peace.

That seems plain enough, and yet little in this history is exactly as it seems. The provenance of this letter, as Caroline Fraser has pointed out, is uncertain. In the best of circumstances it would have arrived in the south too late to save the Fancher party, but whether it was delivered at all is an open question. The Mormons are among the world's most efficient record-keepers, and yet the original of this letter is lost. Brigham Young admits this in a deposition given in 1875. A copy, sworn to and notarized by Nephi W. Clayton, turned up in a church letter book in 1884; but Hamilton Gray Park, one of Brigham Young's assistants, made a note claiming that the letter was in answer to a plea from the south for instructions as to what to do about the Fancher party.

The request for instruction and Brigham Young's answer were both entrusted to the courier James Haslem, who sped from the south to Salt Lake City and then back to the south, a distance said by some to be a round-trip of 496 miles, which he made in one hundred hours. Assuming that relays of horses were made available that does not seem especially fast to me, although Young had pleaded with the courier to ride night and day, insisting to Haslem that "that company [the Fancher party] must be protected from the Indians if it takes every LD Saint in Iron County to do it."

There are problems in regard to Brigham Young's letter and Hamilton Gray Park's memo about it that historians have so far not convincingly explained.

Was Brigham Young, relieved of the immediate threat of attack by the U.S. Army, sincere in his desire to save the Fancher party? Though the army was delayed, it was still coming; might it be that he wanted to be careful not to give them a new excuse to invade? However cynical he may have been about the immigrants themselves, he might not, at this juncture, have wanted to throw fuel on a smoldering fire.

Of course it's possible that this famous letter might not have been the only message he dispatched to the south. The nice letter may have been intended as cover in case things went wrong.

In an army report made by Major James H. Carleton (the same officer, who, just a few years later, commanded Kit Carson to go round up the Navaho), it was stated that the Paiute chiefs claimed that letters ordering the destruction of the emigrant train came from Brigham Young. The copious and meticulous Mormon archives are absent any such letters.

Where one stands on the several vexed questions having to do with the Mormon leader's involvement in the destruction of the Fancher party finally depends on what one believes about Brigham Young himself. The letter of September 10 instructing Elder Haight not to meddle with the immigrants could be shrewd political disinformation, something he could show to the army to prove his good intentions, if that became necessary. All his urgings to the fast rider, Haslem, could have sprung from the same motive. He wanted to appear to be doing his best to save the immigrants. Did he know that Haslem couldn't possibly get there in time?

On the other hand, once told of the massacre, not long after it happened, Brigham Young is said to have had the immediate and uncomfortable intuition that this massacre was something that would haunt the Mormon church forever — which, so far, it has.

He had this intuition, and then, for eighteen years, did his best to stonewall — and his best, considering his lofty position, was pretty good. Though he was told in some detail by Jacob Hamlin and John Doyle Lee what had happened at Mountain Meadows, he publicly insisted, for nearly two decades, that the Indians had done it, not the Mormons. It was only in 1875, in a deposition, that he finally admitted when he knew what he knew. It is clear that he used the power of his position as church leader to keep the truth from coming out, a practice that has been followed by many church leaders since.

Brigham Young had been aware of the Fancher party for some time. Had he wished, he would not have needed to wait until the last minute to instruct Elder Haight not to molest them.

The corresponding question that might be asked is whether Elder Haight and the Mormons of remote southern Utah would have executed all these travelers without the explicit approval of Brigham Young and the other Mormon authorities in Salt Lake City.

My own feeling about this is that the Iron County Mormons were raring to go for the immigrants. No doubt they would have welcomed a go-ahead from Brigham Young, but Salt Lake City was a long way off; the Iron County Mormons were in a mood to kill, and kill they did, on that plain with the seductive grass.

Doctrinally, in the eyes of the Mormon leaders, the majority of the immigrants — that is, the adults — were *not* innocents. They were, in Mormon terms, gentiles, enemies of the faith, perfect candidates for the enactment of blood atonement.

The council of elders held in southern Utah before the attack contained few if any moderate voices. What the elders seemed mainly to concern themselves with was rounding up enough Indian allies to help them at their bloody task. This proved not hard to accomplish — the sight of all those cattle was enough to tempt the Paiutes. Once the Fancher party paused to graze their herds, the stage was set; the Mormons and the Indians were ready.

Early on the morning of September 7, while the immigrants were at breakfast, the firing began.

Mountain Meadows
(II)

The Fancher party, as I have said, was no pushover. Once bullets started whizzing into the breakfasting camp the wagons were immediately circled. Soon formidable breastworks were constructed. Had the party been camped a little closer to a nearby spring, so as to have an adequate water supply, they might have mounted a lengthy siege. The Paiutes did not like long battles, preferring to overcome their enemies in a wild rush or else pick them off one by one over a long stretch of time.

Though several immigrants were killed in the initial attack, the immigrants held off this first assault. They had not made it all the way from Arkansas to fold at the first sign of trouble. Also, they were not long in observing that a number of the "Indians" who were attacking them showed patches of white skin underneath their war paint. The attacking party probably numbered about 250 strong: two hundred Indians and perhaps fifty white people. They were not strong enough to overrun the barricade of wagons and breastworks. Butchering and booty-gathering were obviously going to take some time. Council had to be taken and taken quickly. The battle took place on an established trail. Other immigrants might show up, and, even if they didn't, the Paiutes might tire of the siege and drift off to other pursuits.

The immigrants, of course, soon recognized that they were in a bad situation, in a remote and pitiless place. When night fell they sent scouts to the west, hoping that they might slip through to California quickly and bring help.

None of these scouts made it through. A statement the leaders had composed, describing the desperate situation, was lost with the scouts.

The Mormons were by then fully determined to eliminate the immigrants, but how? A long siege was out of the question; their allies the Paiutes would run off as many cattle as possible and then vamoose. Soldiers might show up along this much used route; soldiers, or merely other travelers.

After some praying and much discussion, the Mormons concluded that the best strategy would be to decoy the immigrants with a promise of safe passage. They would be told that if only they would disarm they would be allowed to proceed in peace. The arrangement would be for each male immigrant to hand over his weapons and then walk out with a Mormon escort. The women and children could walk ahead.

Here one has to step back and attempt to understand why the leaders of the Fancher party fell for this transparent ruse. They were not fools; they had come a long way through dangerous country. Why would they simply take the word of these white men, some of whom had been shooting at them over the course of three days? White men, moreover, who had taken the trouble to paint themselves up like Indians? That in itself should have registered as a bad sign; perhaps it did. The Fancher party had no reason at all to trust either the Indians or the Mormons. They knew quite well that the latter hated them, because of where they came from and because they were gentiles.

Were there not those in the party who questioned the wisdom of unilateral disarmament while surrounded by their foes? Did no one manage to foresee what was coming?

The question can't be answered — not with any certainty. Either the Mormon negotiators were exceptionally persuasive, or the immigrants felt their position to be so hopeless that they would grasp at any straw. Perhaps the members of the Fancher party simply could not believe that white men would massacre them and their women and children. Also, they may have had no clear idea as to how large a force they were in conflict with.

Seventeen young children survived this massacre, but none of the men who made the decision to disarm was spared. Any opinion one might have about the decision-making would only be guesswork; but, still, the ease and speed with which they accepted the Mormon offer seems inexplicable. The siege was only in its fourth day. The fate of the scouts dispatched to California was not yet known.

Perhaps crucially, they could not reach the nearby spring without exposing themselves to rifle fire: perhaps it was thirst that tipped the balance.

What we now know is that on the morning of September 11, after a not especially prolonged parley, wagons were brought forward in one of which the armed immigrants were to stack their weapons. This they meekly did. Then the menfolk of the Fancher party were marched out, each man with an armed Mormon by his side. The women and children were somewhat ahead of the men, having marched out first. The Indians remained in hiding.

These women, having lived under conditions of terror for four days, were likely not free of fears about what would happen if the Indians were allowed to have their way. Perhaps, like the men, they reposed their hopes in Mormon decency. The historian J. P. Dunn suggests that they had even begun to perk up — it's not clear to me how he could know this. He thought, from what reports I don't know, that the womenfolk had begun to regain their confidence; if so, they didn't regain it for long.

Suddenly Major High Higbee, the military man who devised the Mormon battle plan, appeared on a ridge ahead of them. Major Higbee waved his arms and shouted something like Do-Your-Duty, whereupon the Mormon escorts immediately shot down the men they had been escorting. The few who failed to die immediately had their throats cut, so that, Dunn suggests, the atoning blood could flow more freely. (For whatever reason, a great many throats were cut during the massacre.)

According to Dunn, the Indians then fell on the women and children — they had been assigned the job of killing these tender ones, presumably to avoid the possibility of some Mormon shedding innocent blood. A baby had already been killed by the same bullet that cut down his father, who was carrying him at the time, a death that threw an instant taint over the whole gory enterprise.

The long-held view that the Indians took care of the women and kids received a severe challenge with the discovery of the mass grave at the massacre site in 1999. When those bones were uncovered the Mormon authorities must have felt at least briefly that the place was cursed. Thanks to the abundance of Native American remains in Utah, there were laws on the books protecting just such a discovery. With the help of the then governor, Mike Leavitt, a descendant of a massacre participant, and, of course, the Mormon hierarchy, these laws were eventually evaded, but not before a dedicated team of forensic scientists had had some time to work — and *did* they work, eighteen hours at a stretch; they were well aware that the powers that be would soon succeed in having those telltale bones reburied.

This, of course, is exactly what happened, but in fact the scientists still prevailed, assembling parts of twenty-eight individuals and piecing together eighteen skulls.

It was the skulls that cast most doubt on the old belief that the Indians had done most of the killing. Most of the males whose skulls were reassembled died of gunshots fired at very close range — the females, in most cases, had been bludgeoned. The close-range executions by pistol shot suggested white behavior rather than Paiute behavior. The Paiutes had long claimed the Mormons did the lion's share of the killing. Thus what had begun as an attempt to landscape the monument site had blown up in the Mormons' faces. The Paiutes were not entirely exonerated but the notion that they had more or less been slackers at this massacre gained currency again.

Whichever group, Mormons or Indians, accounted for the largest share of the dead did nothing to lessen the horror of what had occurred that September day. Terrible violence occurred, a terror in the desert. Many of the women were quickly dispatched but some children fled. Two young girls hid in some bushes, only to be spotted, dragged out, raped, and killed. One of them pled for her life but John Doyle Lee, the man eventually executed for his role in the massacre, cut her throat anyway. (Lee maintained that he killed no one, but various witnesses said otherwise.)

Seventeen children — innocents in Mormon terms, which meant that they were seven years old and under, were spared and, at first, divided among Mormon families. Most of them were eventually retrieved and sent back to Arkansas — twenty years later their testimony came back to haunt the perpetrators.

John Doyle Lee, Philip Klingensmith (a Mormon bishop), and Jacob Hamlin all insist that they reported the massacre to Brigham Young as soon as it was practicable to do so. The prophet seems much shocked by the killing of women and children, but he then made this remarkable statement about that grisly aspect of the affair:

I have made that matter a subject of prayer. I went right to God with it, and asked him to take the horrid vision from my sight, if it was a righteous thing that my people have done in killing those people at Mountain Meadows. God answered me, and at once the vision was removed. I had evidence from God that he had over-ruled it all for good, and the action was a righteous one, and well intended.

Brigham Young evidently spoke those words to John Doyle Lee, and went on to say that he had heard from Mormons who took part in the killing with Lee, concluding that "we will look into that."

He certainly did look into it, firmly insisting for the next eighteen years that the Mormons had no part in the massacre; it was not until he gave his deposition in 1875 that he admitted to being an accessory after the fact. When he finally got around to visiting southern Utah he even ordered the destruction of a cross that had been erected at the site of the killings. (The Mormons have had extremely bad luck with monuments on that site — if you count the first crude cross, the present monument is, I believe, the fourth to be erected; perhaps the reason for the bad luck is that — except for that cross — all have been dishonest, erring, always, by omission.)

The Mormon God was certainly a most forgiving deity to so easily cleanse the record of all those women and children, hacked and bashed to death in that remote meadow. Enough gentile blood soaked into the ground that day to atone for a hundred Parley Pratts.

Once the killing was done, the fun part — the looting and divvying up of the immigrants' considerable property — could begin. Six hundred cattle were a fine prize in themselves; John Lee may have gotten as many as two hundred of them. By Arkansas estimates the Fancher goods were worth $100,000; the Mormon reckoning was $70,000. John Lee, who seems to have been the treasurer of the local Mormon polity, actually charged the government $1,500 for property allotted to the Indians.

The bodies of the dead were quickly stripped and searched. Ears were out off, that being the quickest way to get earrings. Fingers were lopped off and rings removed. According to Dunn, all the bloody clothing was for a time piled in the back room of an office in Cedar City, where it soon grew fragrant. It seems that the clothes were referred to locally as relics of "the Siege of Sevastapol," a somewhat surreal touch. Writing in 1886, Dunn suggested that some of the Fancher jewelry was still being worn by Mormon matrons.

★ ★ ★

As I have several times said, massacres
will out, and this one did in spades.
Brigham Young's efforts to contain the
news did not succeed. The pile of naked,
cut-up bodies — in effect a meat mountain
— was soon discovered by a party of men
passing through the same grassy meadow.
Here is one account of what the travelers
found, in testimony later given on the
witness stand:

Saw two piles of bodies, one composed
of women and children, the other of
men. The bodies were entirely nude,
and seemed to have been thrown pro-
miscuously together. They appeared to
have been massacred. Should judge
there were sixty or seventy bodies of
women and children: saw one man on
that pile; the children were from one
and two months up to twelve years; the
small children were almost destroyed by
wolves and crows; the throats of some
were cut, others stabbed with knives;
had bullets through them. All the
bodies were more or less torn to pieces,
except one, the body of a woman,
which lay apart, a little southwest of the
pile. This showed no sign of decay and

had not been touched by the wild animals. The countenance was placid and seemed to be asleep. The work was not freshly done — suppose the bodies had been there fifteen or sixteen days.

The travelers who discovered the bodies gave testimony and were believed. Soon, as J. P. Dunn reports, the news "flew on wings of the wind" to every part of the country. The people of California asked the president for support — the people of Arkansas were forced to wonder if any of their loved ones were alive. Outrage ran high, as it should have, prompting the Mormons to issue various lame statements — they are still issuing them to this day, as witness President Hinckley's evasions at the dedications of the new monument.

The general thrust of these statements, for the first eighteen years at least, was to put the blame squarely on the Indians.

The first lame line of defense was that the immigrants had angered the Indians by giving them a poisoned cow; there was the suggestion that the Mormons might also have poisoned the spring. But when Dr. Forney, the superintendent of Utah, went south to launch an investigation, the Paiutes themselves immediately gave the lie to these accusations. There was no poisoned cow, and the spring ran as pure as ever. (Of course, with so many animals, a cow might easily have eaten a poisonous weed: the cow might have bloated and died; but the Paiutes, no fools, would have been quick to note any such distemper. A bloated cow is hard to miss.)

Dr. Forney had come south predisposed to believe the Mormons, but only a few days on the ground convinced him that the Mormon story was seriously flawed. Kanosh, the leader of the local Paiutes, flatly disputed all the stories of poisoning.

Meanwhile, in the court of public opinion, the fact that the Mormons had let it be known that they intended to defy the U.S. Army did not sit well. The Mormons were rapidly losing the public relations effort, as, in a sense, they still are.

Dr. Forney didn't press his investigation until the summer of 1859, but, though fooled at first, he soon realized that there was something wrong with the Mormon version of the killings. For one thing, the Mormon account and the Paiute account flatly contradicted each other.

The local Mormons, evidently thinking that Dr. Forney would believe any white man over any Indian, foolishly gathered together sixteen of the surviving children and tried to persuade Dr. Forney that they had been with the Indians all along. Both Kanosh and the children themselves denied it, which didn't stop the Mormons from presenting the superintendent with a bill for $1,700, which is what they claimed it cost them to buy the children back from the Paiutes. Somehow it didn't occur to the local Mormons that they wouldn't be believed.

Well, they weren't. Some of the children were now nine years old and quite able to confirm that they had been with Mormons, not Indians, for the past two years. Seven years of age was, for Mormons, the cutoff point between innocence and knowledge. In this case it was the knowledge the children had that made them a threat to the Mormon story line. It was soon apparent that, in producing the children, the Mormons had merely produced so many witnesses against themselves. Several children pointed out that some of the killers were just painted white men. "White hell hounds," Dr. Forney called them; he went on to say that these men had "disgraced humanity."

In the spring of 1859, not long before

Dr. Forney arrived, a company of dragoons and two companies of infantry were dispatched to Mountain Meadows to bury the bodies, which, by this time, were dispersed over a rather large area.

It was Major (later General) Carleton who ordered the rude cross erected at the site of the massacre. He felt he ought to do something to commemorate the victims.

It was this modest marker that disappeared during Brigham Young's visit to the south.

Fifteen of the seventeen children who survived were eventually sent east, first to Fort Leavenworth and then back to Arkansas; two boys who had been retained as witnesses were first taken to Washington and then returned to Arkansas as well. Eventually the U.S. government allotted each survivor 320 acres of land, but, so far as I know, the descendants of the victims have not gotten back any of the monies that the Mormons took from the dead. The descendants, of course, still might try to recover those losses, which is one reason the Mormons are so careful not to admit anything.

While Dr. Forney was pursuing his investigations, an attempt was made to hold a legal court of inquiry in southern Utah, but the attempt had to be abandoned when the U.S. Army refused to provide protection for the witnesses, who considered that they would be committing suicide to testify without such protection. When Brigham Young finally came south with would-be judge John Cradlebaugh, Young is reported to have this to say about Mormons who don't support the official story:

> I am told that there are Brethren who are willing to swear against the Brethren who were engaged in this affair. I hope there is no truth to that report. . . . But if there is I will tell you my opinion of you and the fact so far as your fate is concerned. Unless you repent at once of that unholy intention, and will keep the secret of all you know, you will die a dog's death and be damned, and go to hell. I do not want to hear anymore treachery among my people.

Warrants had apparently been issued for some participants, but when the army declined to provide protection the warrants were set aside.

Some of the Mormons who had gotten

away with being painted white men in the slaughter of the Fancher party soon tried it again on smaller groups of immigrants. There were at least four copy-cat attacks, involving rape, gougings, deaths of babies, in which painted white men were involved.

Soon, though, the dead of Mountain Meadows began to exercise their potency. Some of the participants wasted away; and the site itself, where grass had once grown belly-high to a cow, became sere and desolate, as it is today.

More than a decade passed after the first truncated attempt at an inquiry with little change. At this time, in Utah, the selection of jurors was still a prerogative of the Mormon church. Once Congress undid this, there was at least some hope of effective prosecution. John Doyle Lee was first brought to trial in 1875, in a proceeding that smacked of farce. Lee was sure that the church would protect him, and, for a time, it did, despite the fact that former bishop Philip Klingensmith, who had long since removed himself to California, came back, testified, and told the whole story. His testimony was corroborated by several witnesses, despite which a mostly Mormon jury promptly acquitted Lee.

Nevertheless, with this farce of a trial, the always shaky edifice of the Mormon cover-up began to crumble. Details of what happened at Mountain Meadows were soon known to the whole country — the media era had arrived. The testimony of Klingensmith and others fatally undermined the attempt to hold the Paiutes responsible for it all.

Somewhat to the surprise of the Mormon church, the national response to this coached verdict was immediate and severe. Suddenly nobody believed the Mormon story. The response, indeed, was so negative that the church did an abrupt about-turn and decided to sacrifice John Doyle Lee.

In their sudden panic the Mormons retreated to one self-defeating legal strategy after another; individual witnesses soon ensnared themselves ever and ever more tightly in the loops of their own previous falseshoods. Talk was one thing, but legal process something else: its coils began to tighten around many confused participants.

By this time Brigham Young himself had been deposed and had admitted that he was an accessory after the fact. Various witnesses who had remembered nothing at the first trial began to realize that they might unwittingly have implicated themselves. In desperate attempts to undo this damage, to free themselves from the coils of the court, they often contradicted themselves wildly; many soon lost track of what they knew and what they believed.

This time John Doyle Lee was speedily convicted and sentenced to death. He was allowed to choose the method of his own execution and he chose to be shot — in 1877, at the massacre site, he was killed by a firing squad.

John Doyle Lee spent his last days either cursing the Mormon church, or confessing, which he did four times, in wild spewings that contained many contradictions. Dunn dryly observes of the second trial that the jury that finally convicted Lee had no more right to sit in judgment of him than had the sultan of Turkey. He was killed by his own people, all of them hoping to save themselves.

Brigham Young, a man who kept many secrets, died peacefully a few weeks later.

J. P. Dunn ends his long account of the Mountain Meadows Massacre with this vivid splash of color:

The Mormons were right in their superstition that a Nemesis stands, ever threatening them, on the mountains of southern Utah. She does stand there, and in her outstretched hands, for the ash branch and the scourge, she holds a curse over the doomed theocracy, while from her ghastly lips comes the murmur of those words which no prophet can still: "Vengeance is mine, I will repay," saith the Lord.

The theocracy was not doomed — it prospers today, but I would have to agree that Nemesis still broods over that massacre site, particularly in the area of the monument they can never get right. In attempting to pretty up the monument site a backhoe operator uncovered a mass grave, the very last thing the Mormons would have wanted to happen. But when it did happen they proceeded to remake laws in order to get the bones back into the ground before the forensic team could do its work, which only makes them seem the more guilty.

Nemesis may not depart, either, unless the Mormon church can somehow bring itself to be honest about Mountain Meadows, and that day has clearly not arrived.

Probably some of the Mormons who put on war paint and slaughtered immigrants did suffer agonies of remorse. Killing people is no light task. But if some few wasted away, quite a number seemed to live with the crime well enough, their discomfort level only increasing during the second trial of John Lee, when many of them had to abruptly change positions that they had been defending for twenty years.

John Doyle Lee had every right to be outraged at the church and the colleagues who sacrificed him. Yet he himself had wiped blood off his hands that day, helped himself to some of the cattle and some of the loot, and lived serenely as a prosperous farmer, for twenty years a well-respected man.

He took the massacre in stride, and so did many of his co-participants. Many of them felt genuinely indignant when they were finally linked to this crime they had committed so long ago. Some may have convinced themselves that they were off hoeing corn that day. A lie sustained for twenty years can come to seem like the truth.

Utah is a state with many fabulous beauty spots: Mountain Meadows is not one of them. It is a long way from anywhere. The monument — perhaps I should say the most recent monument, for who knows what Nemesis will yet wring out of the Mormons? — at least has the names of the victims on it. And yet this monument put up to honor the victims merely insults them yet again in its half-honesty. There are the names of the victims — where are the names of the killers? Unlike the fine memorial plaque at Wounded Knee, the Mountain Meadows monument leaves a bad taste in the mouth. In southern Utah dishonesty still rules; Nemesis is not yet satisfied. The simple cross that Major Carleton put up to begin with would have served mourners better than the present showy fraud.

The Mormons' final argument, once it had been proven by the testimony of Lee, Klingensmith, and others that they had participated in the massacre, was that the Indians made them do it. The authorities tried to argue that the Indians would have killed the Mormons had they not helped in the attack. This lacks even the semblance of probability: the Indians lacked the weaponry to do anything of the sort.

The authors of the most recent studies of this dread event offer different theories as to why the wagon train was attacked.

Sally Denton thinks the principal motive was greed — no wagon train that rich had ever passed that way; the money to be made, the loot to be collected, drew the locals into action. Will Bagley argues that it was not greed but creed: the blood atonement creed.

The participants themselves may have remained defiant for twenty years, but many Mormons were so repelled by what they heard that they left the church. Neither Brigham Young nor anyone else could hold them, a fact that tells us much about the common horror at massive bloodletting.

If one contrasts the amount of commentary on the Sacramento River Massacre with the flood of commentary about Mountain Meadows, one might suspect a racial element in the accounting: whites killing whites attracted more attention than whites killing Indians. There are a dozen books and many historical commentaries on Mountain Meadows and yet I'm not sure that the racial point is valid. Probably the most written about massacre of the nineteenth century was Sand Creek, where, once again, whites were killing Indians. Mountain Meadows involved a theocracy that, due to a resort to terror, had been put on the defensive, whereas

Sand Creek involved trade routes, settlement issues, and racial hatred. Mountain Meadows and Sand Creek both produced more than one official trial or inquiry. Like great battles, big massacres seem to demand repeated reassessments. Why the killing? How many died? Who was to blame? There is always much to be decided, but the way to a sound decision is never very clear.

SAND CREEK,
NOVEMBER 29, 1864

The Sand Creek Massacre site is now on land owned by a Colorado rancher named Bill Dawson — or at least it is unless he's recently sold his holdings. The site is just north of the hamlet of Chivington, Colorado: the town is named, of course, for John Milton Chivington, the man who planned and led the massacre.

The Arkansas River is a little distance to the south, flowing through expensive irrigated agricultural country. Not far upriver is the reconstructed Bent's Fort; it had been the first great trading post on the Santa Fe Trail, visited by everybody who traveled this famous trail. William Bent, who, with his brother Charles and the trader Ceran St. Vrain, built the original fort, which had initially been farther west, had a number of half-breed children by two Cheyenne sisters: first Owl Woman, who died, and then Yellow Woman.

At least four of William Bent's children were camped with their Cheyenne cousins on the day of the Sand Creek attack: Robert, George, Charles, and John. What happened that day turned one of these sons — Charles — into a half-crazed, white-hating Dog Soldier, a torturer and killer who at one point even went south meaning to kill his own father. Fortunately William Bent was away at the time.

Bill Dawson, the rancher who owns the land where the massacre occurred, is, by all accounts, a reasonable and likable man who, while holding his own views on Sand Creek, has nonetheless been generous with Indian groups who want to hold prayer services there. In the 1990s he allowed Connie Buffalo, an Ojibwa woman who had come into possession of two scalps taken at Sand Creek to bury them at the site, with appropriate ceremonials. Connie Buffalo had been given the scalps by the owner of a small motel near the site. They had been in the man's family for years but the owner seemed to feel that Connie Buffalo had a better right to them: he offered them to her with tears in his eyes.

I mention this exchange because it suggests that the power of such an event as Sand Creek resonates through time as few other experiences do. Southeastern Colorado, like much of the Great Plains, is very thinly populated now. There are not many people there, but most of the farmers and ranchers who operate near the site had been in that place for a long time. Sand Creek, whether they like it or not, has always been in their lives. Some might still argue for Chivington's position, but few doubt that the tragedy marked their families and their region. Few, I imagine, see it as a simple case of white wrong. Though it *was* wrong, it had a context that few not of that region can appreciate now.

I would agree with the locals that Sand Creek wasn't simple. Perhaps the plainest thing about it was the character of John Chivington, who, though a longtime Free-Soiler, was also a racist Indian-hater. But Chivington was not the only man shooting Indians that day and Sand Creek was not an entirely spontaneous eruption of violence, in which some hotheads in Denver decided to attack a camp of one hundred percent peaceful Indians.

When I visited Sand Creek, the best I could do without bothering Mr. Dawson was to drive around it in a kind of box route, on dirt roads. From several rises I could see where the massacre took place. On much of my box route I was trailed by an SUV from Michigan — its occupants no doubt hoped I would lead them to this historic place. I couldn't, and they finally drove off down the road toward Kansas, which is not far away.

The country around the site is rolling prairie — very, very empty. From several modest elevations I could see the line of trees where the fighting took place. The plain is immense here; on a chill gray day the word "bleak" comes naturally to mind. "Pitiless" is another word that would apply. On a fine sunny day the plains country of eastern Colorado looks beautiful, but Sand Creek and Wounded Knee were winter massacres; the cold no doubt increased the sense of pitilessness. If you were at Sand Creek, being massacred and desiring to run, only the creek itself offered any hope. Otherwise, north, south, east, or west was only open country: totally open.

The first factor that might be noted in a discussion of Sand Creek is the date: 1864. The Civil War was in progress, a fact of some importance, as we will see.

More important, though, was that at this date the Plains Indians, from Kiowa and

Comanche in the south, north through the lands of Arapaho, Pawnee, southern Cheyenne, and the seven branches of the Sioux, were unbroken and undefeated peoples. All were still able, and very determined, to wage a vigorous defense of their hunting grounds and their way of life. Up to this point what they mainly had to worry about in regard to the whites was their diseases, smallpox particularly. Though there had been, by this point, many skirmishes between red man and white, there had been only one or two serious battles.

The first major conflict occurred about a decade before Sand Creek, at Fort Laramie. The U.S. government called an enormous powwow, in which the various Indian tribes were to be granted annuities if they would agree not to molest the growing numbers of immigrants pouring west along the Platte — what we call the Oregon Trail. The natives called it the Holy Road.

The expectations the government nursed about this hopeful arrangement were wholly unrealistic — it involved a major misunderstanding of Native American leadership structures. No Indian leader had authority over even his own band such as a white executive might possess. No Indian leader was a boss in the sense that General Grant was a boss. And, all Indian leaders had trouble with their young warriors, who *would* run off and raid.

But few whites recognized these realities at the big gathering in 1854.

Shortly after this great powwow a foolish and arrogant young officer named Grattan took the part of a Mormon immigrant who claimed that a Sioux named High Forehead had killed one of his cows — a crippled cow, it may have been; it may even have been an ox.

High Forehead belonged to the Brulé Sioux, the branch then led by a reasonable chief named Conquering Bear, who at once offered to make restitution for the cow. He may even have offered the Mormon a couple of horses; but Grattan insisted on High Forehead's arrest. Conquering Bear pointed out that High Forehead was a free Sioux: he himself had no authority to order an arrest.

At this point Grattan, determined not to lose face, shot off a small field piece, killing Conquering Bear, something even Grattan probably had not meant to do. The Sioux then immediately killed Grattan and thirty of his soldiers, including the fort's interpreter, who may have contributed to the disaster by exceptionally sloppy translation. The Sioux could probably have destroyed the Fort Laramie garrison at that point, but they chose, instead, to take their dying chief and melt away.

About a year later the army mounted a punitive expedition led by General William Harney, who went north and attacked a band led by Little Thunder, who had not been involved in the trouble at Fort Laramie. General Harney too had field pieces, and used them to slaughter many Sioux — about ninety, some say, an enormous loss for the Indians. This may have been the battle that showed these Western tribes the true killing power of the whites. Crazy Horse may have witnessed this slaughter and decided as a result to have nothing to do with white men, other than to kill them.

A second large-scale conflict prior to Sand Creek was the Great Sioux Uprising in Minnesota in 1862, a conflict that occurred because the Sioux in southeastern Minnesota were being systematically starved by corrupt Indian agents who refused to release food that they actually had in hand. The rebellion led by Little Crow was so fiercely fought and had so many victims on both sides that for a time it retarded emigration into that part of the country. The Indians were eventually defeated, but not before they killed many whites and brought terror to the prairies. When it was over the whites prepared to hang three hundred Indians, but Abraham Lincoln took time out from his war duties to study the individual files, reducing the number hanged to about thirty.

If one considers the Plains Indians as they were in 1864 — a mere twelve years before the Little Bighorn — they constituted a formidable group of warrior societies, all of them naturally more and more disturbed by the numbers of white people who surged across their territory, disrupting the hunting patterns upon which their subsistence depended.

In Colorado, where Sand Creek happened, emigration soared in the 1850s because of gold discoveries in the Colorado Rockies. This brought many thousands of people into the region in only a few years, and yet the Indians tolerated this great wave of whites pretty well at first. Denver was organized as a town in 1858; it was a rough community from the start, and its physical situation, at the very base of the

Rockies, meant that it could only be reached from the east by crossing a vast plain; the natural terrain offered little protection. On that plain, in 1858, grazed millions of buffalo, the support of the nomadic warrior societies mentioned above. Soon freight routes across the prairie bisected the great herds and eventually more or less split them into northern and southern populations. The emigrants came in all sizes and shapes; there were large freight convoys bringing in much needed goods and equipment, but there were also single families traveling alone, struggling across the great emptiness in hopes of finding somewhere a bit of land where they could sustain themselves. If the 1850s were largely quiet, with neither the Indians nor the immigrants knowing quite what to make of each other, by the early 1860s Indian patience had begun to wear thin.

There began to be attacks, sometimes on a few soldiers, more often on the poorly defended immigrant families. From around 1862 on, immigrant parties that happened to run into Indians were apt to be roughly treated, the men killed and mutilated, the women kidnapped, raped, butchered. The meat shop attitude had clearly arrived on the Great Plains. The government built forts, here and there, but these the Indians could easily avoid. The forts offered little protection to the widely scattered immigrant parties.

Pioneering during this period was always a gamble, no matter which route one took across the plains. By the early 1860s all routes into Denver from the east were dangerous. Hundreds of miles of plain had to be crossed, with the immigrants vulnerable to attack all the way. But the westering force was irresistible in those years and the immigrants kept coming.

In Denver, every time a wagon train or immigrant family got wiped out, local temperatures rose. *Apprehension,* which I have earlier suggested as a factor in several massacres, became acute in Colorado during the first years of the 1860s. In the little towns and even in Denver women were oppressed by fears of kidnapping and rape. Every depredation got fulsomely reported. One captured woman, after a night of rape, managed to hang herself from a lodgepole; others survived to endure repeated assault and, in some cases, eventually escaped to report details of their ordeals.

John Milton Chivington was a Methodist

preacher from Ohio. In New Mexico, at the Battle of Glorieta Pass, he became a Union hero by flanking a force of Confederates who had moved up from Texas; the Confederates lost most of their supplies and were forced into ignominious retreat. A major at the time, Chivington was made colonel and soon brought the authority of a military hero into the bitter struggle with the Plains Indians.

Some historians argue that the Confederates skillfully exploited the hatred of the plains tribes in order to increase pressure on Union troops. It is certainly true that in Oklahoma the Five Civilized Tribes, or such of them as had survived the Trail of Tears, fought mostly with the Confederates. The famous Cherokee general Stand Watie was, I believe, the last Confederate officer to surrender, which he did on June 23, 1865, well after Lee had had his talk with Grant.

No doubt there had been some deliberate provocation by the Confederates in Texas and New Mexico, but it's hard to believe that many of the Plains Indians much cared which side won this white man's war. What kept *them* stirred up was the whites' rapid invasion of their country.

In the decade following the Fort

Laramie conference an ever-increasing number of smart Indian leaders saw very clearly the handwriting on the wall. Many of these had been taken to Washington and New York; they had seen with their own eyes the limitless numbers of the whites, and the extent of their military equipment. Many of these leaders came to favor peace, since the alternative was clearly going to be destruction. The problem was that even if Black Kettle — who led the band attacked at Sand Creek — strongly favored peace, that didn't mean he could then exercise full control of his warriors. Leadership among the plains tribes was collective but never coercive. Black Kettle and other leaders commanded a good deal of respect but it didn't gain them much control. Warrior societies, after all, encouraged aggressive, warlike action. Raiding, for the young men, was more than a sport: it was how they proved themselves.

In the late summer of 1864, some two months before Sand Creek, the army and the Colorado authorities organized a council in an attempt to arrive at some kind of peace policy that might work. If the various tribes could endorse such a plan, and if they kept their word, they would be promised protection from attack. The peace Indians could even be given some token — a medal, a certificate, even an American flag, which would enable soldiers to distinguish them from hostiles while on patrol.

This ill-formed policy only increased the confusion, and there had been plenty of confusion already. Many bands were eager to become peace Indians and get their medals, irrespective of whether they seriously intended to stop raiding.

At one time not long after the conference it was rumored that six thousand Indians were on their way to Fort Lyon to sign up for the new program. No doubt the figure was wildly inflated. Even six hundred Indians would have swamped Fort Lyon and exhausted the supply of medals, if there were any medals.

John Chivington attended this strange council, which he regarded, not unjustly, to be a fraud and a sham. Black Kettle and a number of other chiefs readily acknowledged that there was likely to be a problem with the young warriors, besides which there were the Dog Soldiers, renegades from many bands who saw themselves as defenders of the old ways — they intended to keep fighting no matter what. Bull Bear, a leading dissident, attended the council but was so disgusted by what he heard that he stormed out, vowing to fight on — he fought on, and died at Sand Creek.

Of all the leaders of the southern Cheyenne, Black Kettle seemed the most sincere in his determination to live in peace with the whites. In fact he was sincere to the point of naïveté. He had been given an American flag in 1861 and had acquired a white flag as well, both of which he waved frantically to no effect as Chivington and his men rode down on the camp.

In the weeks before Sand Creek, the routes into Denver came under increasing pressure from roving bands of Indians, and every attack or small conflict merely strengthened Chivington's hand. Soon enough, with Governor John Evans's consent, a poster was printed asking for volunteers to fight the Indians. The volunteers were to serve for one hundred days — Chivington easily raised a sizable force, but, in casting his net wide, he took with him a number of men, such as young Captain Silas Soule, who were not convinced of the necessity of the proceedings. Several such men were opposed to massacre as a method of control. Some of the men, particularly those under Silas Soule, refused to fire when the time came: some, including Soule, testified against Chivington in the rather unhelpful inquiries following the massacre.

Even so, Chivington had plenty of firepower and an abundance of converts. He was six foot four and his towering presence easily cowed such waverers as dared to question the operation. Chivington was no coward. Twice in his career as a fire-breathing minister he had faced down formidable opposition, sometimes preaching with a loaded revolver on both sides of his pulpit. The congregation's objection was probably to his Free-Soil, anti-slavery belief, convictions that are to his credit and which he never abandoned.

Just as intensely as he longed to free the slaves, Chivington also longed to exterminate the Indians, even unto the women and children. Well before Sand Creek he had been quoted as saying "Nits breed lice." General Sherman, for a time at least, shared this view. And in fact no effort was made to spare the women and children at Sand Creek, at least not by the troops operating directly under Chivington's command.

As with all massacres, there are puzzling lacunae in the many narratives of the survivors. How far from Sand Creek was Fort Lyon, from which the expedition set out at 8:00 p.m. on the evening of November 28? Some thought it was forty miles, some thought thirty, and others said merely "a few."

The vast company troop, somewhere between seven hundred and one thousand men, left the fort under cover of darkness, so that their movements would not be detected. Of course, had there been any Indians in the vicinity who were not stone-deaf they would not have needed to see much to know that a large body of men was on the move. The troops were traveling with artillery, which by itself would have made a good deal of clatter. The fact that, however far they came, they were in position above Black Kettle's camp at dawn on the 29th suggests that they pressed on at a good clip through the night.

Controversy lingers about the scouts that led Chivington and his men across that darkling plain. One was the half-breed scout Jack Smith, who so ran afoul of Chivington that he was executed after the battle. Another was the old mountain man Jim Beckwourth, who lived to testify against Chivington at the inquiry; whether he witnessed the whole battle is disputed. And there was Robert Bent, son of William, who, some think, was forced to lead Chivington to the camp. If so Robert Bent must have been quite uncomfortable with what was happening, since he knew that various of his siblings were likely to be in the camp. All the Bents survived, though George received an ugly wound in the hip.

In the first predawn moments when the troops began thundering toward the camp, some of the Cheyenne women thought a buffalo herd must be nearby. They soon learned better. Chivington and the troopers always maintained that a Cheyenne fired first; if so, it was a lonely effort. About two-thirds of the Cheyenne in camp were women and children — there were perhaps fifty or sixty warriors. What saved the survivors were the steep creek banks, in which the fighters among the Cheyenne at once began to dig shallow rifle pits. The steepness of the banks enabled some to flee southeastward without exposing themselves to a fusillade from the troops. That the surprised Cheyenne managed to put up any resistance at all is a testament to their fighting spirit. Not for nothing did George Bird Grinell call them the "fighting Cheyenne."

Young Captain Silas Soule immediately infuriated Chivington by refusing to order his men to fire; he even briefly interposed his troops between the Indians and the volunteers. Some say the ensuing battle lasted from dawn until mid-afternoon; others say the mopping-up operation continued all day. The few warriors who survived the first assault dug their rifle pits deeper and fought bravely to cover the retreat of those who fled beneath the creek banks. Black Kettle's wife was shot nine times, and yet, when darkness fell, he carried her to Fort Lyon, where the doctors saved her.

Various stories from this battle exist in so many versions that they have become tropes. One involved a little Indian boy who stood watching the soldiers. One volunteer shot at him but missed; a second volunteer announced that he would "hit the little son-of-a-bitch," but he too missed. A third took up the challenge: he didn't miss.

Another often-told story involved a wounded Indian woman who held up her arms beseechingly, hoping to be spared; but, like the old, bloody-eyed woman in the Odessa Steps sequence of *Battleship Potemkin*, she was hacked down.

The Cheyenne fought gallantly, well into

the afternoon — a few of the warriors managed to slip away. When the firing tapered off, the looting began. As at Mountain Meadows, fingers and ears were lopped off, to be stripped of rings and ornaments. Almost every corpse was scalped and many were sexually mutilated. A kind of speciality of Sand Creek was the cutting out of female pudenda, to be dried and used as hatbands.

Chivington and his men returned to Denver, to celebrity and wild acclaim. The scalps — one hundred in number — were exhibited in a Denver theater. Chivington, very much the hero of the hour, claimed to have wiped out the camp.

In fact, though, quite a few Cheyenne and Arapaho survived Sand Creek, including all of William Bent's sons. The Indians hurried off to tell the story to other tribes, while the one-hundred-day volunteers celebrated.

Chivington's most fervent admirer, Colonel George Shoop, confidently announced that Sand Creek had taken care of the Indian problem on the Great Plains — his comment was the prairie equivalent of Neville Chamberlain's famous "peace in our time" speech, after Hitler had outpointed him at Munich. Shoop was every bit as wrong as Chamberlain. Sand Creek, far from persuading the Indians that they should behave, immediately set the prairies ablaze.

It sparked the outrage among the Indian people that led inevitably to Fetterman and the Little Bighorn. The Indians immediately launched an attack against the big freighting station at Julesburg, in northeastern Colorado. But for another blown ambush by the young braves, they might have wiped out the station. As it was, they killed about forty men. The trails into Denver that had been dangerous enough before Sand Greek became hugely more dangerous.

In the twelve years between Sand Creek and the Little Bighorn there were many pitched battles. Some, like Custer's attack on the Washita in 1868, in which Black Kettle and his tough wife were finally killed, went to the whites; others, such as Fetterman or the Battle of the Rosebud, went to the Indians. All up and down the prairies, from the Adobe Walls fight in Texas to Platte Bridge in Wyoming, a real war was now in progress. Charles Bent became one of the most feared of all Dog Soldiers, killing and torturing any whites he could catch.

★ ★ ★

In Denver, Chivington's account of the raid did not go long unchallenged. In this case the power of the dead began to make itself felt almost at once. Stories soon seeped out about the terrible mutilations of women and children. People who had fully approved the attack — people tired of apprehension, of being afraid even to venture out of town for a picnic, were nonetheless troubled by some of the horrors they heard about. Stories about mutilated children — despite the "nits breed lice" doctrine — did not play as well as they had at first.

Reports that the Indians hadn't wanted to fight were shouted down by the Chivington mob, but they kept leaking out. The carnage began to sit heavily on certain consciences, as it usually does after massacres. There had been a few soldiers, like Silas Soule, who refused to shoot down helpless Indian women or their children; in time some of them expressed their disgust at the proceedings. Chivington's supporters were well in the majority, but there *was* a substantial minority opinion and it did get expressed.

Even as the battle began there had been doubters who informed Chivington that the Indians were trying to surrender; but he brushed this aside. He did not want to hear from Indian sympathizers and was not pleased by the least equivocation on the part of his militia. He had gone on a mission of vengeance and he made no bones about that fact. He frequently reminded the soldiers of what had been done to white women in the recent raids, and he succeeded well enough in keeping most of his troops stirred up.

But even Chivington, forceful as he was, did not succeed in banishing all doubt, all regret. The field of battle was one thing; a formal court of inquiry quite another. The formality inherent in even such a crude judicial procedure is about as far as civilized man gets from the dust, smoke, noise, and blood of a battlefield.

The inquiry was ordered by Congress. Once it got underway, Chivington objected to almost every question that was asked. With his towering presence and his power of denunciation he could intimidate many witnesses, but not all witnesses. Silas Soule held his ground and yielded nothing to Chivington's bluster; the preacher made little headway with old Jim Beckwourth either. In the East the greatly respected General Grant gave it as his opinion that what

127

happened at Sand Creek had been nothing more than murder. (He was equally blunt about what happened at the Little Bighorn twelve years later, declaring at once that the tragedy was Custer's fault, a judgment that cannot have pleased the grieving Libbie Custer.)

Despite Chivington's resistance, the commission of inquiry made it clear that what happened at Sand Creek was an out-and-out massacre. Joseph Holt, the army's judge advocate, called it "cowardly and cold blooded slaughter, sufficient to cover its perpetrators with indelible infamy and the face of every American with shame and indignation."

In this the judge advocate clearly went too far, because there were plenty of American faces in Denver who expressed neither shame nor indignation. Neither Chivington nor Shoop was charged with anything; to have charged them at that moment in Denver would have led to civil insurrection.

In April 1865, three weeks after he had married, Silas Soule, the officer whose testimony had done Chivington the most harm, was assassinated while taking a stroll on a pleasant evening. His murderer was most likely a man named Squiers, who promptly fled to New Mexico. The army sent Lieutenant James Cannon to apprehend him, which Cannon accomplished without undue difficulty. Squiers was returned to Denver but escaped again and headed west. This time Lieutenant Cannon could not pursue him because Lieutenant Cannon had been found dead in his hotel room, probably poisoned. Squiers was never brought to trial.

The carnage and ambuscade on the prairies east of Denver did not stop. Julesburg was attacked a second time. Then the Civil War ended, a cessation that forced the military authorities to notice that there was a full-scale Indian revolt going on in the West, conducted by a goodly number of highly mobile and also highly motivated warriors who were, at this juncture, fully determined to prevent the whites from taking their land.

Through the long winding, up and down, of the Indian wars, John Chivington remained popular in Colorado. To the end of his life he defied his critics, declaring, over and over again, that he stood by Sand Creek. He was to have his trials and sorrows. His son drowned and his wife died, after which he quickly married his son's young widow, who soon took herself home. There were allegations of abuse. Chivington moved to San Diego, but soon returned to Denver, where he became an undertaker and, eventually, the county coroner. He died in 1894, about thirty years after the attack that made him famous, or infamous.

More than one Western historian has defended Chivington, one being J. P. Dunn, he of *Massacres of the Mountains*, who makes quite a spirited defense of the fighting preacher and his one-hundred-day volunteers. Dunn calls Chivington "a colossal martyr to misrepresentation." In his polemic Dunn points out, correctly enough, that there was a life-or-death struggle taking place on the western prairies in the early 1860s. The conflict *was* brutal; many immigrants did lose their lives.

It could hardly have been otherwise. The Indians were rapidly being squeezed out of the country that supported them — country they held dear. The tactical problem that the first Denver council tried to address, how to tell a peaceful Indian from a hostile Indian, was never solved. A fighter such as Roman Nose, a war Indian for sure, might nonetheless visit a peace

Indian such as Black Kettle. Plains Indians moved around, visiting for a time with this band or that. The hostile and the peaceful were never to be easily separated out.

After the Fetterman Massacre in 1866, General Sherman made a blunt exterminationist remark. According to H. L. Mencken, it was Sherman, not General Philip Sheridan, who, when approached by an Indian beggar at a railroad depot with the claim that he was a good Indian, replied that the only good Indian *he* had ever seen was a dead Indian.

Sherman was not happy, two years later, at the end of what has been called Red Cloud's War, when the government was forced into its only public retreat in the whole era of this conflict: it agreed to abandon three forts that had foolishly been thrown up along the Bozeman Trail. They had been supposed to protect miners and other travelers to Montana but happened to have been erected right in the heart of Sioux country. With what meager manpower the army had at the time they could not be defended.

The army had, for once, truly over-reached — it had underestimated the power of the tribes. Custer was to make the same mistake at the Little Bighorn.

Once the forts were abandoned, the Indians burned them.

Part of J. P. Dunn's admiration for Chivington stems from the fact that the fighting parson never gave ground. He never tried to shift the blame for Sand Creek to anyone else, or to pretend that he had intended to do anything other than what he did do: kill as many Indians as possible. Dunn's argument is that at this stage of the fighting nothing but merciless cruelty would impress the Indians. He even argued that the mutilations had the same purpose: to convince the Indians that white men could deal in terror as effectively as they themselves could. He felt that the Indians did not respect gentle treatment, though he himself knew that they did respect *fair* treatment.

Dunn ends his defense with one of those purple perorations of which he was so fond:

Was it right for the English to shoot back the Sepoy ambassador from their cannon? Was it right for the North to refuse to exchange prisoners while our boys were dying in Libby and Andersonville? I do not undertake to answer these questions, but I do say that Sand Creek is far from being the "climax" of American outrages to the Indian, as it has been called. Lay not that unflattering unction on your souls, people of the East, while the names of Pequod and Conestoga Indians exist in your books; nor you of the Mississippi Valley while the blood of Logan's family and the Moravian Indians of the Muskingum stain your records; nor you of the South, while a Cherokee or a Seminole remains to tell the wrongs of his fathers; nor yet you of the Pacific Slope while the murdered family of Spencer or the victims of Bloody Point and Nome Cult have a place in the memory of men — your ancestors and predecessors were guilty of worse things than the Sand Creek massacre.

That summary is hard to dispute. The burned-alive Pequots probably did have it worse. The reason Sand Creek gets highlighted is because some of those killed were prominent peace Indians. Black Kettle's peaceful position had been well known for many years, but Chivington didn't care. He attacked the largest encampment he could find — the more militant bands would not have been so easily found, and it's doubtful that they could have been surprised. Black Kettle's band was easy pickings precisely because they believed they were safe. To some extent Black Kettle compounded this lapse when he was attacked and killed on the Washita.

Arthur Penn's rendering of Thomas Berger's *Little Big Man* contains at least three massacres. The first might loosely represent Sand Creek, the second the Washita, and the third the Little Bighorn. If Americans — or even Westerners — remember anything about Sand Creek it is that Black Kettle was frantically waving his American flag as the troopers charged in. Some say his companion White Antelope was holding up a peace certificate when he was shot dead; it is more probable that he was merely making some gesture of surrender. From the point of view of poorly trained or wholly untrained cavalry, that there were a lot of peace Indians in this camp might not have been obvious. Most of the attackers were probably more frightened than enraged, though rage or at least adrenaline arrived quickly enough once the shooting started.

The mutilations the victors performed

were horrible, though not nearly as encyclopedic as those the Sioux and Cheyenne managed to visit on Fetterman's men two years later, in a battle that barely lasted half an hour. Here is what the troops found when they went out to bring in the bodies after the Fetterman wipeout: the words are those of Henry Carrington, at that time commander of Fort Phil Kearny, whose military career was destroyed by this disaster:

Eyes were torn out and laid on rocks; noses cut off; ears cut off; chins hewn off; teeth chopped out; joints of fingers; brains taken out and placed on rocks with other members of the body; entrails taken out and exposed; hands cut off; feet cut off; arms taken out of sockets; private parts cut off and independently placed on the person; eyes, ears, mouth, and arms penetrated with spearheads, sticks or arrows; ribs slashed to separation with knives; skulls severed in every form, from chin to crown; muscles in calves, thighs, stomach, breast, back, arms, and cheeks taken out. Punctures upon every sensitive part of the body, even the soles of the feet and the palms of the hand.

★ ★ ★

Considering the short duration of the Fetterman Massacre, as opposed to the nearly all-day struggle at Sand Creek, the Sioux and Cheyenne made Chivington's men seem like amateurs of massacre, which indeed they were.

The same catalogue could be restated for the Little Bighorn, with the addition of decapitation and a few other refinements. Chivington's hundred-day volunteers were for the most part Sunday soldiers, content with pouches made from scrotums and the like. When it came to making a meat shop they possessed only the crudest skills.

I am not sure that Sand Creek admits of any conclusions. Two peoples with widely differing cultures were rubbing against each other, constantly and insistently. The Indians were trying to defend their cherished way of life, the whites to make that way of life vanish so they could go on with their settling, farming, town-building, etc.

On a world scale countless massacres have been perpetrated over those and similar issues. Land is frequently a principal element in these disputes. Is it my land or your land, our land or their land? Time after time, in the Balkans, India, Pakistan,

136

Kashmir, the Middle East, large parts of Africa, the same concerns develop. Peoples don't seem to be good at sharing land, even when there's a lot of it to share. Where land is in dispute massacres are just waiting to happen — it's only a question of time, and usually not much time at that.

THE MARIAS RIVER MASSACRE, JANUARY 23, 1870

The massacre of Piegan Blackfeet in their winter camp on the Marias River, in what is now Montana, in January of 1870 is unique among the massacres considered in this book.

Why? Because this large band of Blackfeet were dying anyway: of smallpox, at the rate of six or seven per day.

It is not likely that Colonel E. M. Baker, who lead the assault on the Blackfeet camp, knew that the tribe was infected when he set out to eliminate them as a raiding force, but he found out soon enough and went right on with the killing; at the end of the day the army claimed to have killed 173 Indians, a big total.

What was odd about it — apart from the circumstance that the army chose to kill Indians who were dying already — is that the army claimed to have killed 120 warriors, a proportion of warriors to women and children not seen in any other massacre. J. P. Dunn throws up many statistics in order to suggest that the army's count couldn't have been right. There were *always*, in his view, more women and and children to be found in a camp than men.

Well, if they don't have smallpox, maybe. The 120 warriors might well have been in camp because they were too sick to be anywhere else.

But if they were that sick, why bother to kill them?

Because they were Blackfeet — probably the most feared of all Western tribes — that's why.

When Captains Meriwether Lewis and William Clark made their great trek across America and back in 1804–1806 they encountered many Indians, some of them ill-disposed toward the Corps of Discovery; but they got all the way to the Western Ocean without killing a single native, a high tribute to the care they took to get on with the local tribes.

On the return journey they were not quite so lucky. While Captain Lewis and some of the Corps were exploring the Marias River country, not too far from where the 1870 massacre would occur, they traveled for a while with some Piegan Blackfeet, although the Piegans were well known to be brazen thieves.

Sure enough, one morning, a Piegan boldly seized a rifle and attempted to make off with it. The attempt didn't work and, in the struggle over the gun, the Piegan was stabbed to death. Another Piegan fired at Captain Lewis, who shot back, wounding him. Whether he died is debated. The Corps proceeded home; there was no more trouble with Indians — the stabbed Piegan was the only sure kill on the whole amazing journey.

The Blackfeet country is in northwestern Montana and some of Idaho. No group of Indians was more determined to keep whites out of their lands. As early as 1731, when the great Canadian explorer La Verendrye tried to cross from what is now South Dakota to the Western Ocean it was most probably the Blackfeet who turned him back. Travel in the Blackfeet country, from the Yellowstone over to the Columbia, was just not safe.

Indeed, one of the famous episodes in the history of the American fur trade involved the militant Blackfeet. On their way back down the Missouri in 1806 the captains met two intrepid traders who were

140

resolutely setting out to trap in the High West. This intrigued young John Colter, a member of the Corps. He was given permission by the captains to go back upriver and try to keep his hair while he sought his fortune.

John Colter *did* keep his hair, but, upon encountering some Blackfeet, two of his companions were not so lucky. They were killed, but the Blackfeet must have been feeling sporting, because they gave Colter a chance. He was stripped naked and told to run. The Blackfeet allowed him a decent start and then set out in pursuit.

John Colter *could* run. With his life on the line he ran so hard that blood gushed out of his nose. Even so, one fast-running warrior was closing in on him, spear at the ready. Colter whirled suddenly, taking the warrior by surprise. He wrested the warrior's spear away and killed him with it.

Then he ran some more, finally eluding his captor pursuers by slipping into an icy pond and hiding under a beaver dam.

The annoyed Blackfeet finally gave up.

Naked, Colter walked out, through a land of geysers. The likelihood is that he discovered Yellowstone.

The Blackfeet were a handsome people.

141

The first painters who managed to get upriver, to Fort Union or Fort McKenzie, loved to do their portraits and have left us some fine ones.

The painters were the American George Catlin and the Swiss Karl Bodmer. Some of the portraits they did on the upper Missouri between 1832 and 1834 are among the finest examples of Western art.

The relevance of all this to the massacre of the dying Piegans in 1870 is that the militancy of the Blackfeet was well known and widely respected. That particular part of Montana is thinly populated even today, in part because of Blackfeet resistance.

Thus when Colonel Baker arrived at the Blackfeet encampment that morning he killed the raiders he had come to kill. Many of them no doubt would have died, but Colonel Baker was not disposed to leave it to chance, his reasoning perhaps being that those who managed to recover would soon be able to be troublesome again.

When Blackfeet were involved, the U.S. Army would rather be safe than sorry. They had come to kill, and they killed.

THE CAMP GRANT MASSACRE, APRIL 30, 1871

With the exception of the Sacramento River Massacre, Camp Grant seems to have been the least studied of these Western slaughters, though it is certainly remembered in Arizona by all the peoples involved: Apache, Mexican, Papago, and white. Sometimes it's called the Aravaipa Massacre, for the creek north of Tucson where it took place. What distinguishes it from the other killings is that in this case *all* the people killed — excepting one old man and a "well-grown" boy — were women and children. At the Marias River all the victims were sick; at Camp Grant they were either female or young.

The fighting men were not at home.

The Aravaipa band of western Apache were as much feared as the other, more militant, bands, such as those that had been led at various times by Cochise,

Victorio, or Geronimo. Though the Aravaipa leader, Eskiminzin, was a capable raider, the Apaches who eventually settled near Camp Grant were largely semi-agricultural. The commander at Camp Grant at the time, Lieutenant Royal E. Whitman, allowed them to camp near the post but kept them under tight control, counting them every other day and attempting to keep track of their goings and comings. Urged by his superiors, he made some effort to get them to go to the White Mountain Reservation, but they didn't like the White Mountains and refused to go. Some of them became friendly with the local ranchers and helped them cut hay and do other chores.

When the number of these unreservationed Indians swelled to around five hundred, Lieutenant Whitman decided he had better seek counsel from his superiors as to whether he was allowed to grant such a number of Indians de facto asylum. At this juncture a little military surrealism enters the story: Lieutenant Whitman's request for instruction was returned unread because he had failed to summarize his message on the outside of the envelope, a nicety the military code seemed to require.

144

This rejection came in early March 1871. In recent months there had been a number of small-scale attacks well south of Tucson, a good distance from the Aravaipa but close enough to alarm the citizenry of Tucson — white, Mexican, and Papago — to take up arms. The Apache and the Papago were bitter enemies; likewise the Apache and the Mexican.

On the 28th of April Captain Penn at Fort Lowell sent Lieutenant Whitman a message saying that a large and mixed group of men were said to be heading north out of Tucson, in the direction of Camp Grant. The messenger bringing this news arrived at the camp in the early morning of April 30.

Lieutenant Whitman immediately sent some men to the Apache camp to urge the Apaches to come closer to the fort, but when the men reached the encampment they discovered that they were too late. The men from Tucson — six whites, forty-eight Mexicans, and ninety-four Papago — had already done the work they came to do. More than one hundred Apaches were dead — all had been killed with knives, hatchets, or clubs. The Papago, particularly, favored clubs.

A puzzlement to me, at least, is that the

raiders could slip in and destroy a camp this size with no one at the nearby fort suspecting anything. Dunn says the fort was only half a mile from the camp — perhaps it was farther away; otherwise it seems strange that no one or no thing at the fort heard anything. Surely the horses would have been alarmed, or the dogs, or the sentries. Even though the raiders didn't use guns it seems odd that a hundred people could be put to death without breaking the early morning silence. Did no one scream, or no babies cry, or no dogs bark? Lieutenant Whitman had deliberately kept the Indians close so he could monitor their comings and goings.

Besides this, the camp was set afire — did no one smell the smoke and wonder what was going on with the Apaches?

Perhaps Dunn was wrong — the bulk of the Apache camp may have been farther away than he thought; otherwise it's hard to believe that such deadly work produced no outcry at all.

When, later in the day, a doctor was sent from Camp Grant to bring in the wounded, he found very few wounded to attend. The raiders with their knives and clubs had done a very thorough job — though they missed Eskiminzin, the man they wanted most. In fact, they missed all the men. A few women were able to take advantage of the half-darkness to flee; but those who didn't were treated with the usual severity.

Twenty-nine Apache children were taken in this raid; most were sold into slavery in Mexico, a source of great bitterness to the survivors. J. P. Dunn called this massacre "pure assassination," and the succinct President Grant called it "murder, purely."

Grant eventually sent an able investigator, Mr. Vincent Colyer, to Arizona with the legal power to bring the culprits to justice. Once again murder had outed, quickly in this case, but Mr. Colyer soon found the citizens of Tucson to be even more stridently defiant than the Mormons had been after Mountain Meadows or the citizens of Denver in regard to Sand Creek. The Arizona press was flamboyantly pro-massacre. The papers were so violently biased in favor of the killers that J. P. Dunn was moved to speak harshly about them.

But the uproar in the East was just as passionate, and did not subside. To the great outrage of the citizens of Tucson a trial was finally held and 148 raiders were indicted.

The legal proceedings, conducted in

circumstances of high tension, were as farcical as the first trial of John Doyle Lee. The jury took only nineteen minutes to acquit the defendants, surely one of the shortest jury deliberations in the annals of jurisprudence.

But, at least, the light of the law had been shone on the massacre. The atrocities were aired in open court.

Practically speaking, this massacre, like Sand Creek, backfired, intensifying the combat between the Apaches and everyone else. Cochise, the Chiricahua leader who had been living peaceably, went back to his stronghold in the mountains. Fifteen more years of raiding and killing followed.

The Bureau of Indian Affairs, always several steps behind the action, attempted to stabilize the situation by shifting small groups of Indians from here to there, but these efforts mostly stirred the Indians up, rather than calming them down. The situation soon became so volatile that the army was forced to send one of its very best men, General George Crook, to sort things out.

By the time Crook arrived in Arizona the situation with the Apaches was beyond the power of any one administrator to fully correct, but Crook took his time, did his best, and effected some real improvements.

George Crook's career as an Indian fighter and administrator contradicts perhaps more clearly than any other J. P. Dunn's assertion that the Indians only respected merciless behavior. Crook was no softie, of course, but he did try to be fair, and the Indians recognized as much and respected him for it. Custer might have flair, but Crook was solid. His assistant John Gregory Bourke's *On the Border with Crook* continues to be one of the most readable books about this period. Bourke would be the first to admit that Crook was not easy to work with; but his ability was never in doubt.

Unlike most military administrators, Crook took the time to try to understand the differences between the nine branches of the Apache people, from the Mescalero, far to the east between the Rio Grande and the Pecos, all the way west, to the Apaches who lived near the Gila. It was Crook who recognized the folly of cramming disparate and incompatible bands onto the same reservation. He made real progress. Even Geronimo, a particularly hard sell, developed some respect for General George Crook.

Unfortunately for peace in Arizona, Crook's skills and authority soon came to be in even more urgent demand elsewhere: that is, on the northern plains, where Red Cloud and his allies were still proving to be a little too strong for the U.S. Army to subdue. Crook was called north and given a sizable command, perhaps too sizable, because it slowed his power of maneuver. In the main he was less effective in the north than he had been in Arizona. His all-day battle on the Rosebud, a week before the Little Bighorn, was no army triumph; but for the bravery of his Crow and Shoshoni scouts it might have been a very bloody defeat.

In Arizona, absent Crook's calming hand, the situation failed to improve. The army and the Bureau of Indian Affairs muddled and then muddled some more. Eventually, well after his inconclusive pursuit of the victors at the Little Bighorn, Crook was sent a second time to the Apacheria, his main task being to catch Geronimo, though Geronimo was by no means his only problem. By 1882, when George Crook returned to the Southwest, many Apaches were off the reservation, doing as they pleased. Crook had to do some hard campaigning, in very inhospitable places; but he did eventually get many of the Apache bands back on more or less suitable reservations.

At one point Crook almost reeled in Geronimo, but that slippery fellow developed second thoughts: he went out one last time. Crook had done most of the work, but it was General Nelson Miles who eventually took Geronimo's surrender.

It had been Miles, also, who accepted the famous surrender of Chief Joseph of the Nez Percé, in the Bearpaw Mountains, not far from Canada, to which the Indians were headed in their long and dramatic flight.

Miles would have dearly loved to take Crazy Horse's surrender too — that would have given him an enviable triple — but this was not to be.

It is nearly impossible to calculate, at this distance, how many deaths occurred in the Apacheria between the Camp Grant Massacre and Geronimo's surrender. Camp Grant turned out to be a particularly pointless massacre, in which the least threatening Indians in the region were killed. Like most massacres, it proved to be counterproductive. The outrage it spawned just led to more fights. Papago-Apache strife was not new — it had been going on ever since the two people had begun to inhabit the same country; and, likewise, the strife between Apaches and Mexicans. Old hatreds were involved — to some degree they still are.

As in Colorado, the influx of white people into arid southern Arizona was partly due to rich mining possibilities. The geologist Raphael Pumpelly, who came to Arizona because of the mines, has some excellent descriptions of white-Apache conflict in his travel book *Across America and Asia.*

According to Pumpelly, the Apaches found the Americans laughably bad as fighters. In the north the Sioux and Cheyenne held the same opinion. Some of Major Reno's men, at the Little Bighorn, were so obviously terrified that the Sioux and Cheyenne youth split their sides laughing as they chased them down. According to Pumpelly the western Apache found the white man's attempts at warfare so laughable that they let them live, so as to have a good laugh another day. Geronimo, who did not appear to have much of a sense of humor, probably would have killed them.

★ ★ ★

The issue of the twenty-nine children taken in the Camp Grant raid rankled for years. Once they were across the border, it was virtually impossible to recover stolen children.

Though much vilified in the Arizona press, which claimed that he debauched with native women, Lieutenant Whitman was a decent young officer who had done his best to help the local Apaches, whom he had come to like. Some of the ranchers in the area had begun to soften toward the Apaches too, employing them when they could. What was lost as a result of the massacre was the small, fragile measure of trust that the two peoples were beginning to develop for each other. This trust had only been possible because of Whitman, a calm, sensitive administrator.

In time a good many Apaches came to trust Crook, who fought them hard when he fought but who had never been an exterminationist. Once he had subdued a given group of Indians, he did his best to secure decent treatment for them.

The Aravaipa leader Eskiminzin lost two wives and five children at Camp Grant. He fled into the mountains and did not come

153

back. He also may have taken revenge when an opportunity presented itself. J. P. Dunn, who liked statistics, reckoned that there were fifty-four attacks by Apaches on whites following Camp Grant, which is more or less what happened after Sand Creek. When Crook returned to fix what could be fixed, Dunn had this to say about the difficulties he faced:

It must be remembered that he had left to him a legacy of hatred of three centuries between the people he had to pacify; that a large proportion of the white population were as barbarous in their modes of warfare as the Apaches themselves; that Arizona was still a refuge for the criminal and lawless men of other states; that war and pillage had been bred into the Apache, until they were the most savage and intractable Indians in the country; that large bands of their nation infested northern Mexico, and had almost impenetrable strongholds there; that Mexico still pursued war in the old way and still paid bounty for Apache scalps, no matter where procured; that slaving still existed in Mexico, and it was next to impossible to recover Indians once carried over the line.

★ ★ ★

All true. The president's man, Mr. Colyer, did a conscientious job of trying to sort things out, but the local white power structure was wholly hostile to him; for a long time the situation remained unsatisfactory and unsettled. Apaches, like most people, naturally have a strong preference for their own particular kind of country, whether desert, mountain, or plain. Shuffling them around from one poor reservation to another seldom improved anybody's mood; and yet remnants of that system are evident in Arizona today.

Red Cloud's old remark about the white man promising to take their land and then taking it is everywhere evident in Arizona. As soon as a given bunch of Apaches, attempting to make the best of a bad situation, began to adapt to one reservation, likely as not they would be shifted to another.

If the Apaches succeeded in making a given location cultivatable, then the whites would inevitably want it.

Neither General Crook nor his successor, Colonel Kautz, liked this way of doing things; but they were soldiers, not bureaucrats; and by this time management of Native American affairs came more and more to be the domain of bureaucrats. In the end the Indians always lost. What applied to Red Cloud, Spotted Tail, Sitting Bull, Quanah Parker, or Crazy Horse turned out to apply, as well, to Cochise, Victorio, Geronimo, and the rest.

In the Southwest this pattern has been established as far back as 1863, when some soldiers captured the Apache leader Mangus Coloradas, killed him, and cut off his head. That the struggle then continued for more than twenty years was mainly because Geronimo — the last of the desert Apache leaders — was far from easy to catch or kill.

In the end, though, as was to be the case from sea to shining sea, the whites had better equipment, and always prevailed.

THE BROKEN HOOP:
1871-1890

The two decades between the Camp Grant Massacre in 1871 and the final carnage at Wounded Knee Creek at the very end of 1890, were years in which the Indians of the West, from southern Arizona and northern Texas all the way north to Canada and west from the Missouri River to the lava beds of northern California, where the Modocs mounted their final, futile resistance, slowly lost their freedom, their land, and their way of life.

Though there were brilliant victories — Fetterman, the Rosebud, the Little Bighorn — the contest was always unequal and its end inevitable.

The whites — the people with the better equipment — won. Most of the fighting Indians whose names have survived in popular memory — Captain Jack of the Modocs, Chief Joseph of the Nez Percé, Quanah Parker of the Comanches, Red

157

Cloud and Crazy Horse of the Oglala Sioux, Sitting Bull of the Hunkpapa, Spotted Tail of the Brulé, Cochise and Geronimo of the Apaches, fought, died, or surrendered during this period.

Captain Jack was hanged in 1873.

Chief Joseph, after declaring that from where the sun stood then he would fight no more, forever spent the rest of his days in places he did not want to be.

Crazy Horse, the most inspired of all the Sioux warriors, was killed at Fort Robinson, Nebraska, a victim in the main of his own people's jealousy. Without quite realizing it, he had become too big a star.

Sitting Bull of the Hunkpapa took his people to Canada for a few years, but received no help and finally came back and surrendered. He was killed by native policemen on the Standing Rock Reservation while resisting arrest. His death occurred about two weeks before the massacre at Wounded Knee.

Quanah Parker of the Quahadi (Antelope) Comanche surrendered in 1875 and became an effective leader of his people during the painful years of transition from free life to reservation life.

Red Cloud, the Sioux's most able negotiator, lived until 1909 and died in his bed, a wise but not a happy man.

Spotted Tail, cautious leader of the Brule Sioux (and Crazy Horse's uncle) was also killed by one of his own people.

Geronimo, the Apache warrior who held out the longest, surrendered in 1886 and died at Fort Sill, Oklahoma, also in 1909.

Quanah Parker died in 1911, also at Fort Sill.

A number of distinguished military men had their careers defined by the efforts they made in the West to bring the Indian wars to a close.

The most famous of these of course was George Armstrong Custer, who died at the Little Bighorn, his great folly, with a smile on his face.

George Crook did honest service, both against the northern tribes and the desert Apache. He died in 1890, without having to witness the shame of Wounded Knee. His old adversary Red Cloud remarked, almost fondly, of Crook: "He never lied to us. His words gave the people hope."

One of the most able Indian fighters of all was Ranald Slidell Mackenzie. He fought far out on the Staked Plains, where few officers dared to go. In 1875 he broke the power of the Comanches and was sent north to help out with the northern tribes. On the day when he was supposed to be married, Ranald Slidell Mackenzie went permanently insane.

A fourth able leader was General Nelson Miles, who fought in Texas in the Red River War and then went north with Mackenzie. Miles chased both Sitting Bull and Crazy Horse with mixed success, but he survived and, as I said, took the surrender of both Chief Joseph and Geronimo — although, in both cases, he did little of the chasing.

The three chiefs who more or less mastered the diplomatic skills necessary to deal with the white officials and their bureaus were Red Cloud, Spotted Tail, and Quanah Parker; the latter was the half-white son of Cynthia Ann Parker, the most famous of the Comanche captives.

Sitting Bull, who hated the whites from first to last, was surly, impatient, and never a particularly good negotiator. The only white he unstintingly admired was Annie Oakley, his "little sure-shot." Sitting Bull also came to have some respect for Buffalo Bill Cody, in whose show he appeared for a season. Cody, the great showman, in one of his rare understatements, called Sitting Bull "peevish."

In fact the great Hunkpapa was a good deal more than peevish. Even at the very end of his life he still so frightened the whites that, when the Ghost Dancers began to dance and he refused to stop them, the authorities sent the Indian police and some cavalry as well to bring him in.

Though the time between the Camp Grant Massacre and Wounded Knee was almost twenty years, it only took about a half-dozen of those to essentially defeat the Plains Indians. Geronimo was a special case, protected by a harsh but helpful environment.

The government made treaties and broke them constantly. Most of the Indians knew how little chance they had; they knew, if from nothing more than the rapid disappearance of the buffalo, that their way of life was gone. The gathering at the Little Bighorn was their greatest conclave, and their last. They wiped out the arrogant Long Hair and then just melted away, into the vast spaces of the West. With the possible exception of the Fort Laramie council in 1854 they had never gathered in such numbers and they never would again.

After Custer the whites made a great outcry for vengeance, but it was not easy to find Indians to wreak vengeance on.

Buffalo Bill, by then a showman, rushed back west and took what he claimed was the first scalp for Custer, that of the Cheyenne warrior Hay-o-wei, or Yellow Hair. Whether or not Cody actually killed Hay-o-wei is not absolutely clear, but he *did* take the man's scalp, which he sent to his estranged wife as a trophy, hoping it would somehow mollify her. Understanding of the ways of the female heart was not one of Cody's strengths.

General Crook, the gray fox, with a huge contingent of some four thousand men, lumbered around the northern prairies for a while, finding no one to fight. General Miles chased Sitting Bull to Canada but had to let him go. In the dreadful winter of 1876–1877 Crook did hit a Cheyenne village, on a night so cold that eleven babies froze to death.

General Miles switched his attention to Crazy Horse and harassed him into the depths of the winter, but didn't catch him. In the spring Crazy Horse concluded that, for a time at least, the game was up. He came in, with nine hundred people and a lot of horses.

Not long after the army disarmed Crazy Horse, the Nez Percé roared out of Idaho

162

into Montana and made for Canada, mopping up everyone who got in their way. The army, horrified by this unexpected outbreak, seems to have briefly concluded that Crazy Horse might be the only man who could stop them. Bizarrely, as it must have seemed to him, they offered to arm him again if he would go fight the Nez Percé. The offer must have confused him — if he understood it. Puzzled, perhaps, he may have said okay, he would go fight the fugitives until every last Nez Percé was killed. The interpreter at this council, Frank Grouard, who knew Crazy Horse and may have been jealous of him, apparently told the white officers that Crazy Horse had intended to fight until every last white man was dead. Some of the listeners who understood Sioux were horrified; they tried to persuade the officers that Crazy Horse hadn't said anything of the sort, but a dark doubt had been planted in the officers' minds, the fruit of which was the decision made by General Crook to arrest Crazy Horse at once and have him shipped to the Dry Tortugas, to the dreadful prison for incorrigibles.

As is well known, when an effort was made to arrest him, Crazy Horse resisted and was bayoneted by a white soldier, while Little Big Man — once his friend, now an Indian policeman — held his arms.

Crazy Horse died in 1877. The years between his death and 1890 were sad and unheroic times for the native peoples. As it was in Arizona, so it was in Wyoming, Nebraska, and the Dakotas. The government was constantly trying to position these defeated, demoralized people in places where they would do the least harm; this meant, in most cases, allocating them the worst land — even though what at first seemed the worst land soon enough turned out to be land that the whites thought they might just have a use for after all. Few places in the whole West turned out to be so bleak that the whites wouldn't eventually want it.

There was little happiness among these reservationed peoples. There were a few decent, honest Indian agents, but there were many more who were corrupt, interested only in greasing their own palms at their wards' expense. J. P. Dunn rightly excoriated this all too numerous breed.

Then, in the 1880s, out of the desert places, there arose a prophet, a messiah of sorts, who soon began to attract a following; he preached a message of Renewal and Return, to be achieved through a dance ritual that came to be known as the Ghost Dance, since one of its purposes was to have the dead rise up.

This prophet was a short, stocky Paiute named Wovoka — though when he lived with a white family, as he often did, he introduced himself as Jack Wilson. Wovoka, or Jack Wilson, lived into the 1930s — he may even have appeared in a silent movie.

The doctrine he preached — mildly, it should be said — the doctrine of a Return, common to many preachers of various faiths, nonetheless set the stage for the final conflict at Wounded Knee Creek.

Why it should have been thus is a complicated story.

WOUNDED KNEE,
DECEMBER 29, 1890

The anthropologist James Mooney, the author of what is still the classic monograph on the Ghost Dance, happened to be on the southern plains when the massacre at Wounded Knee occurred. Mooney was a pupil of John Wesley Powell at the newly formed Bureau of American Ethnology, one of Powell's personal fiefdoms.

James Mooney had come west specifically to investigate the ritual dance that caused the problem at Wounded Knee. When the first rumbles from the north occurred, he heard them. Mooney had chosen to begin his investigations into the origin and nature of the Ghost Dance in what is now Oklahoma, where he talked with Arapaho, Kiowa, Comanche, Apache, Caddo, Wichita, and other people, all of whom could be met with easily on the southern plains.

I doubt that Mooney was surprised to

166

hear that the Sioux had taken up the Ghost Dance, though I doubt that he supposed such a spasm of violence would result.

When violence flared, James Mooney found himself drawn into an ambitious, multitribal study of the Ghost Dance, soon producing a study called *The Ghost Dance Religion and the Great Sioux Outbreak of 1890*, which appeared as Part II of the Fourteenth Annual Report of the Bureau of Ethnology.

Very fortunately, for students and historians, James Mooney happened to be in the right place at the right time, *and with the right training* — training enough, at least, to allow him to make some sense of what happened on the northern plains in the second half of 1890. In the course of a century or more, his work has often been criticized, but Mooney is still where one must start in attempting to understand how these troubles started, and why.

Mooney's analysis was more than an attempt to explain the government's catastrophic reaction to the Ghost Dance as practiced at the end of the 1880s by the Sioux. He wanted, first of all, to set the Ghost Dance in a universal context, for notions of a return to a time of happiness and plenty hardly just belonged to

Wovoka. Many peoples dream of a return to a time when life was good rather than bad.

In the course of his study Mooney provides a fairly full account of millennial beliefs among native people in all parts of North America. He starts his survey with the preachings of a Delaware prophet in the 1760s, but other scholars have since gone further back. James Wilson, in *The Earth Shall Weep*, an excellent one-volume history of Native American life, claims that the Pamunkey leader Nemattanew was preaching a millennialism not unlike the Ghost Dance as early as 1618, by which date the more astute native leaders had already figured out that these palefaces were a problem not likely to go away. Visions of Eden, as Mooney notes, are woven into the religion of many peoples.

My aim here is to describe how a massacre came to occur, not to write an essay in comparative religion. What is relevant is the power of the desire to return to happier times, a longed-for event often brought about through the appearance of a messiah. Tecumseh's brother, Handsome Lake, preached some such doctrine, and — nearer in time to Wounded Knee, so did the Apache prophet Noch-ay-del-klin, who lived near Cibecue Creek in Arizona, where he was killed, along with a number of his followers, by soldiers who thought his preachings were stirring up the natives they wanted to settle and subdue. Noch-ay-del-klin was only one of many preachers to get in trouble with the civil authorities. Mooney finds elements common to the Ghost Dance in a number of nineteenth-century faiths: Beckmanites, Jumpers, Shakers, Ranters, etc.

I find it broadly interesting that in the last quarter of the nineteenth century, natives in at least four parts of the world kicked out their white invaders in a final surge of native powers. All had intense dancing as a means of preparation; all felt that if they danced fervently enough they would become invulnerable to bullets. (This belief still surfaces occasionally.) The four groups were:

> The Boxers in China.
> The Mahdists in the Sudan.
> The Zulus in South Africa.
> The Sioux and other tribes
>   in North America.

The Boxers were convinced of their invulnerability as they marched on the trapped legations; the Zulus believed it as they prepared their triumphant ambush at Islandwanda; the Mahdists believed it as they faced Kitchener's guns at Omdurman; and the Sioux believed in it in South Dakota — some wore Ghost Shirts that were to keep the bullets from finding them.

Though himself never a disciple of Wovoka — he was much too hardheaded (as was Geronimo) — it is worth remembering that just before the Battle of the Little Bighorn, Sitting Bull stared at the sun and danced until he fainted. When he was revived he at once reported a vision of soldiers falling upside down into camp; and soon enough Custer and his men *did* fall into camp, after which the victorious warriors could sing "Long Hair [Custer] returns no more."

All these native victories were to be *last* victories; none of the four groups were ever to triumph on such a scale again. By the time Wounded Knee occurred — fourteen years after the Little Bighorn — the likelihood of the Sioux mounting any really serious resistance to the U.S. military was small indeed. But the soldiers and the Indian agents had not yet managed to rid themselves of *apprehension* should a given group of Indians stir at all: the old habit of always fearing attack had not yet died out.

Wovoka began to export his Ghost Dance principles to various delegations from tribes that wanted to know about it; but he was, after all, only one prophet, and he was exporting only his version of this hopeful creed. Other prophets, over in Oklahoma or down in Arizona, might be practicing variations, and these Wovoka saw no reason to oppose. Some of these he may never have known about, but he doesn't seem to have considered that he had the only answer.

What remains, for me, the biggest question is why this dancing scared the authorities, particularly the military authorities, so much. The Sioux were poor and weak — what could a little dancing hurt?

Wovoka wrote a number of messiah letters — Mooney reprints three, none in any way militant. The three differ only in syntax. Here is one in which Wovoka, signing himself Jack Wilson, speaks in his own name:

When you get home make a dance to continue five days. Dance four successive nights. On the last night keep up the dancing until the morning of the fifth day, when you must bathe in the river and disperse to your homes. You must all do in the same way.

I, Jack Wilson, love you all and my heart is full of gladness for the gifts you have brought me. When you get home I will give you a good cloud [rain] which will make you feel good. I give you a good spirit and give you all good paint. I will want you to come again in three months, some from each tribe there [Indian territory], there will be a good deal of snow and some rain. In the fall there will be such a rain as I have never given you before.

Grandfather [a universal title of reverence among Indians and here meaning the messiah] says when your friends die you must not cry. You must not hurt anybody or do harm to anyone. Do right always. It will give you satisfaction in life. The young man had a good father and mother [possibly he refers to Casper Edras, the young Arapaho who wrote down the message of Wovoka for these delegates].

Do not tell the white people about this. Jesus is now upon the earth. He appears like a cloud. The dead are all alive again. I do not know when they will be here, maybe in the fall or in the spring. When the time comes there will be no more sickness and everybody will be young again.

Do not refuse to work for the whites and do not make any trouble when you leave here. When the earth shakes [at the coming of the new year] do not be afraid. It will not hurt you.

I want you to dance every six weeks. Make a feast at the dance and have food that everyone may eat. Then bathe in the water — that is all. You will receive good words again from me sometime. Do not tell lies.

Jack Wilson

That would seem to be very mild preaching, and preaching, moreover, that contains a number of Christian elements. There are other Wovoka/Jack Wilson prophecies in which he speaks of a great flood that will drown all the whites and just leave Indians to people the earth — a rather Noah-like prophecy. Dee Brown, in *Bury My Heart at Wounded Knee*, quotes him as saying that Indians who don't dance will "grow little, just about a foot high, and stay that way." After all, Wovoka was a preacher and few preachers deliver the same sermon time after time, with no variation. In none of the sermons I've seen does Wovoka suggest that the Indians take up arms. He himself was very attached to the Wilson family and didn't seek trouble; he suggests that the whites will all be taken care of by the Great Spirit, after the Return.

Why did the instructions of this mild prophet, one who only asks for good behavior, make the whites in Dakota so deeply apprehensive?

At first, in fact, they *weren't* apprehensive. Two experienced agents, Valentine McGillycuddy and James McLaughlin, both told the military, at first, that the Sioux were behaving well: these expert opinions were simply overruled. General Miles also, at one point, thought the situation was well under control. But, despite this opinion, the army kept bringing in troops, which can have only alarmed the Sioux, who had shown no tendency to fight for about ten years. They were weak and poorly fed. Why did this doctrine out of the desert provoke such a terrible massacre?

A part of the answer, I think, was the government's fitful, inconsistent policy of moving Indians from one reservation to another at the least sign of trouble. In virtually every move the Indians lost a little — or a lot — more of the land they held so dear. In 1876–1877 they lost the Powder River country and the Black Hills — the latter their sacred place. As one result of Red Cloud's war the Black Hills had been granted to the Sioux people in perpetuity in 1868; but very soon afterward General Custer discovered gold there. Perpetuity turned out to be a matter of some four years.

The government debated endlessly and schemed and chiseled dishonestly time and again, as they came up with ever more ingenious ways to get this suddenly valuable land away from the Sioux. (In Oklahoma, a few decades later, much the same thing went on when black gold — oil — was discovered in vast quantities on Indian land.)

When waves of immigrants began to sweep into the Dakotas in the 1880s it became necessary once again to find land for them, which usually meant whittling down what the Indians had been allotted. This constant revision of land rights reached all the way down to Indian territory, in what is now Oklahoma, where the Five Civilized Tribes, having already been dispossessed of their Eastern lands, soon found themselves being dispossessed a second time of some of the good land they had traveled to along the Trail of Tears.

In 1877 the northern Cheyenne under Little Wolf and Dull Knife found that they could no longer endure the low, muggy Oklahoma reservation they had been exiled to for whatever role they played in the defeat of Custer. They announced their intention to return to their homeland in Montana, and they went, making the epic march described by Mari Sandoz in *Cheyenne Autumn*, a story later filmed by John Ford. Only half of them made it back, still a remarkable effort, considering that most of the soldiers in the West were chasing them. The Cheyenne version of this epic march was related to me by a tribal elder, Mrs. Elk Shoulders, in Lame Deer, Montana, in the early 1980s, about a century after the Cheyenne made their great march.

Throughout the 1880s particularly, the Indians were frequently pushed into lands they didn't like, onto reservations they came to hate, in order that incoming white pioneers would have places to settle. In the Dakotas the Great Sioux Reservation at first extended to the 104th meridian; eventually the boundary was moved back to the 103rd.

All this occurred while the authorities were still trying to coax Sitting Bull back from Canada. The old man by this time was practiced in resistance, but finally he did come south, and was soon hired by Buffalo Bill to appear in his Wild West Show. Sitting Bull lasted only one season.

Of the Indian leaders still active at this time Sitting Bull was the one the white authorities feared most. He was able, and his dislike of whites — excepting only Annie Oakley and Buffalo Bill — was as evident as it had always been. (Another exception was the Brooklyn philanthropist Catherine Weldon, who seems to have fallen in love with Sitting Bull. At least she lived with him for a time. The nature of this union kept everyone wondering. Agent James McLaughlin, who was in charge of Sitting Bull, insisted that the relationship "wasn't criminal," but the historian Robert Utley has mentioned that there is evidence that suggests otherwise. Mrs. Weldon's young son died of lockjaw while she was ministering to the Sioux.)

Wounded Knee

(II)

Once Sitting Bull established himself on
the Standing Rock Reservation, the same
agent, James McLaughlin, got along with
him about as well as any white official
could expect to. There had been a long,
complicated debate about whether the
Sioux should sell the now much coveted
Black Hills. When asked to mediate, General Crook gave the Sioux some blunt advice: the Indians might as well take the
money, because the whites were certainly
going to take the Black Hills, holy or not.

As the fall of 1890 edged into winter on
the northern plains, a general apprehension seemed to grow, both in Indians and
whites. It is hard to say why. The Ghost
Dance might have some kind of millennial
implications, but it was just a dance held
by some poor Indians — and Indians, like
the whites themselves, had always danced.
Despite these dances the Sioux were still a

very subdued people. The two agents, McGillycuddy and McLaughlin, as well as General Miles, continued to insist that there was no cause for alarm, although McLaughlin did allow as to how the dancing kept the Indians a little "stirred up," the very condition the military authorities found to be the most frightening. More troops were readied, to put down this nonexistent revolt.

Though apprehensive about the troops, the Ghost Dancers kept dancing. The Sioux Short Bull went into the Badlands, where he intended, in private, to dance as much as he pleased. Quite a few tribesmen decided to go with him.

When feeling even slightly nervous about conditions at Standing Rock, agent McLaughlin had a tendency to put the blame on Sitting Bull. In the fall of 1890 the increased presence of soldiers was naturally nervous-making for the Indians. The Indians got the sense that they were going to be punished yet again, though no one knew why and no one wanted to be punished. More and more Sioux adopted Short Bull's tactic and drifted off to the Badlands or the hills.

It took almost no movement on the part of the Sioux to frighten the settlers.

Agent McGillycuddy, who, as a doctor at Fort Robinson, had treated Crazy Horse's wife, was not a man easily panicked. Apropos the Ghost Dance, he made the reasonable point that even the Seventh-day Adventists put on strange robes and performed strange rituals in *their* wait for the coming of the Messiah. Why shouldn't the Sioux be granted the same license?

Agent McGillycuddy's reasonable opinion did not prevail. The army was alarmed, and so a plan was made to arrest the usual suspect, Sitting Bull. General Miles reasoned that if a bunch of white soldiers rode in to arrest Sitting Bull there would very likely be a violent protest, perhaps even a revolt. Miles's first notion was to summon Buffalo Bill Cody, whose show was then in Chicago, in hopes that Cody could coax Sitting Bull to join him for a special performance of some kind. If Sitting Bull agreed, then he could be arrested somewhere off the reservation and sent to a military prison.

It doesn't seem likely that Cody had been informed about this plan; after all, he employed more than one hundred Indians in his show. If he had assisted in the arrest of their most renowned chief it is doubtful that the Wild West Indians would have approved. They might even have revolted themselves, perhaps killing a few of the cowboys and stagecoach drivers that they routinely chased in the show.

Cody may have sensed, or found out, what the real plan was. On his own he made his way to Standing Rock; but then agent McGillycuddy objected to allowing Sitting Bull and Cody — in his view two slippery characters — to get together. Cody was told there could be no meeting, after all; in a huff the great showman went away without ever seeing his old star.

Sitting Bull had last talked to Crook in 1889. Since then he had been living quietly. McLaughlin knew that arresting him would be tricky: it would require great care. He thought it might be accomplished through the use of Indian policemen, of which by this time there were a goodly number. The young men of the Sioux may have regarded their policeman jobs as status symbols.

When the day of the arrest came no fewer than forty native policemen went to Standing Rock to arrest the old man. They were under the command of a Lieutenant Bullhead. As an extra precaution a detachment of cavalry went with them.

The native policemen arrived early, perhaps hoping to whisk the prisoner out before the camp was really awake. Sitting Bull himself was still asleep. Once awake, though grumpy, he finally agreed to go to the agency — it was not the first time he had been so summoned. The arresting officers were Lieutenant Bullhead and Sergeant Red Tomahawk.

By the time Sitting Bull got dressed and stepped outside, a big crowd of Ghost Dancers had gathered. Seeing that he had crowd support, Sitting Bull suddenly balked. He appeared to change his mind. The old show horse that Buffalo Bill had given him was waiting, but Sitting Bull suddenly dug in his heels, forcing the policemen to push him toward his horse. Angered by this treatment of their leader, a Sioux named Catch-the-Bear whipped out a rifle and shot Lieutenant Bullhead, who shot back, hitting Sitting Bull. Red Tomahawk also fired, hitting Sitting Bull in the head. Sitting Bull fell, dead. At this juncture fierce fighting broke out between the Ghost Dancers and the native policemen. The nearby cavalry, hearing sounds of battle, came rushing in and managed to save most of the native policemen, who otherwise would probably have been slaughtered to the last man.

The old show horse, some say, took the shooting as his cue and went through his repertoire of tricks while the battle raged.

Dee Brown and others have argued that it was only the power of belief in the Ghost Dance, with its promise of a Return, that kept a general revolt from flaring up. Some Sioux may have hesitated on that score, but, with Sitting Bull dead right before their eyes, many merely felt leaderless and fearful. Sioux by the hundreds soon fled the Standing Rock Reservation and made their way to the camp of the strongest surviving chief, in this case Red Cloud, who was at the Pine Ridge Agency.

Other frightened Sioux fled to the Badlands, where Short Bull still was. Others went to the mountains. Still others flocked to the other Ghost Dance sites.

Not many seemed to want to stay in the place where Sitting Bull had been killed, a place where worse might follow.

Perhaps as many as one hundred Standing Rock Sioux made their way to the camp of Big Foot, a well-respected Minniconjou chief.

Big Foot was then camped east of Pine Ridge, near Cherry Creek.

WOUNDED KNEE

(III)

Two days after Sitting Bull's death, the army issued a warrant for the arrest of Big Foot himself. The old chief had done nothing hostile at all; he was merely on the arrest list, with many others, as a possible fomenter of trouble. In the eyes of the military he was an enemy combatant, much like the unfortunate Afghans who are being held in Cuba today.

What made this arrest order particularly inconvenient was that Big Foot was seriously ill. He had pneumonia, and was hardly able to stand, yet he was traveling in an open wagon, in wintertime. He was spitting blood; his shirt was stained with it.

On December 28 he saw some cavalry approaching and immediately ran up a white flag. The commanding officer of this troop, Major Samuel Whiteside, insisted that Big Foot and his band come with him to the large cavalry encampment on

Wounded Knee Creek. The major wanted to disarm the Indians then and there, but a half-breed scout named John Shangneau persuaded him to wait until the Indians were safely in camp.

Once in the camp the Indians were carefully counted: 120 men and 230 women and children. Major Whiteside had by this time realized that Big Foot was seriously ill; he had a heated tent prepared for him and sent an army doctor to attend him.

Sometime after dark more soldiers arrived. Colonel James Forsyth took over the command, with orders to take Big Foot and his followers to a military camp near Omaha, a goodly distance from Wounded Knee Creek.

By morning Big Foot was very sick indeed; he was barely able to breathe. His people, now entirely surrounded by soldiers, were naturally very fearful.

The next morning Colonel Forsyth ordered all the Sioux to assemble, so the process of disarming them could begin. Though not happy with his order, the Sioux began, rather tentatively, to comply.

(From this point on, it is only fair to say, there are many versions of what happened, all made by participants.)

The army, with its propensity for taking

things too far, too fast, began to search the tents and the baggage in them, confiscating knives and hatchets as they went. Not many rifles were surrendered, and most of the ones handed over were defective in varying degrees. One of the few good rifles belonged to a Sioux named Black Coyote (or Fox), who brandished his gun above his head and informed the crowd that he had paid good money for it, an indication of his reluctance to part with it.

In the opinion of a witness named Dewey Brand, Black Coyote did intend to turn in his gun and was just having a little fun, but opinions as to Black Coyote's intentions are numerous. One Sioux thought Black Coyote to be a man of bad character. The soldiers were hustling Black Coyote away when his rifle evidently went off — perhaps an accident. Some think no one was hurt, others think an officer was either killed or wounded.

Whatever the truth of that, the well-primed soldiers — most of them members of the 7th Cavalry — began to fire indiscriminately into the mass of Indians. Big Foot, the sick chief, was killed by the first volley. The Sioux then began to fight with what little they had to fight with — knives, clubs, etc. Some of the soldiers who had been carrying out the disarming fell in hand-to-hand fighting.

Next, a Hotchkiss gun opened fire. This fire would seem to be as dangerous to the soldiers as to the Indians on the flats and, indeed, some of the soldiers were in danger from friendly fire. The marker at Wounded Knee says that 146 Indians were killed: the death toll for soldiers is usually thought to be between twenty-five and thirty-one. The Indians began to flee — many were cut down. A blizzard was on the way. When the firing finally stopped most of the wounded Indians were gathered up and taken to the Pine Ridge Agency, where they were housed in the mission.

James Mooney believes that when the sun rose that morning neither the soldiers nor the Indians were expecting trouble. This seems hard to believe. The Sioux were surrounded by soldiers. A machine gun was trained on the camp.

There were more than one hundred warriors with Big Foot. Mooney says a Ghost Dancer named Yellow Bird blew on an eagle-bone whistle and may have danced a few steps. In Mooney's account the Sioux at first relinquished only two rifles, prompting the provocative search of tents and baggage. Mooney thinks Yellow Bird may have told the Sioux that if they were wearing their Ghost Shirts the bullets would not find them. Mooney isn't sure what may have gone on between Yellow Bird and Black Coyote. No one is sure whether the latter fired accidentally or on purpose, or whether he wounded an officer or what.

Once the soldiers began to fire into the crowd, a frenzy developed that was not much different from the killing frenzies at the other massacres. Fear, nervousness, blind rage all contributed to a force that was soon unstoppable. The Sioux either fought or fled, and were hunted down in either case. Some got as far as two miles from the point of eruption before they fell. Mooney thinks Yellow Bird may have egged Black Coyote on, but did he? The point, if there is one, is that in situations of high tension it takes only one vague, perhaps accidental, action to start a violent spasm of killing.

All the ingredients for catastrophe were there: the armed and jittery soldiers, a group of frightened, nervous, much harassed Indians. Perhaps Black Coyote meant to fire his gun, but then perhaps not. He was being shoved around — the shot *might* have been accidental.

At the other massacres — Sacramento River, Mountain Meadows, Sand Creek, Marias River, Camp Grant — massacre was the whole point of the engagement. But at Wounded Knee it seems that it really could have gone differently. A peaceful surrender might have been carried out. But a gun went off, and then many guns went off in response, and, before long, dead human beings littered the plain.

As with Sand Creek and Camp Grant, the ferocious violence at Wounded Knee bred violence elsewhere; for a short time there *was* a revolt among the Sioux, a great many of which were camped near Pine Ridge. Some immediately went into fighting mode; there were a number of ambushes and small attacks. Colonel Forsyth and his troops came under strong assault and might have fared badly had not reinforcements arrived. For some three days after Wounded Knee confusion reigned — confusion mixed with terror. There was plenty of trouble in the south, and yet, at the same time, Indians who had not yet heard of Wounded Knee were trickling into Pine Ridge.

On New Year's Day 1891, a party of soldiers was sent to the battlefield, charged with burying the dead and bringing in such wounded as had survived the battle and the subsequent blizzard. Mostly the soldiers found dead bodies, and yet four babies were found alive, and also a woman named Blue Whirlwind and her children. The dead bodies were stripped and thrown into an open pit. "It was a thing to melt the heart of a man, if turned to stone . . . to see those little bodies shot to pieces," one witness reported.

A little girl was found wearing a cap with a beadwork American flag on it. She lived.

A cowboy named Henry Miller seems to have been killed in the first battle. Why he was there in the first place is not stated.

For Red Cloud it was a particularly anxious time — he was afraid his own hotheads might go out, undoing all he had accomplished in his years of diplomacy.

A Negro private, W. H. Prather, of the 9th Cavalry, wrote a lengthy poem about the battle:

The redskins left their agency,
    the soldiers left their post
All on the strength of an Indian tale
    about Messiah's ghost
Got up by savage chieftains to lead
    their tribes astray,

But Uncle Sam wouldn't have it,
for he ain't built that way.

Private Prather was only outdone in eloquence by Black Elk, the Oglala sage:

I did not know then how much was ended. When I look back now from the high hill of my age I can still see the butchered women and children lying heaped and scattered along the crooked gulch as plain as when I saw them with eyes still young. And can see that something else died there in the bloody mud and was buried in the blizzard.

A people's dream died there. It was a beautiful dream . . . the nation's hoop is broken. There is no center anymore and the sacred tree is dead.

James Mooney's book contains pictures of the children who survived: Marguarite Zitkala-noni, Jennie Sword, Herbert Zitkalazi, and the children of Blue Whirlwind. Captain Colby of the Nebraska State Militia adopted one little girl; Lost Bird, she was called. George Sword, the captain of the Indian police, adopted another little girl, who was called Jennie Sword. One boy, Herbert Zitkalazi, was adopted by Lucy

Arnold, a teacher at the agency. Herbert was the son of the medicine man Yellow Bird, he of the eagle-bone whistle.

Confusing claims circulated and still do. The many descendants of the dead tell the stories they heard, and the stories differ.

Spotted Horse claims that Black Coyote did fire the first shot and that it killed an officer. Others insist that the shot missed.

American Horse, who had been at the Fetterman massacre and even claimed to have cut Fetterman's throat, said that he had seen a mother shot down while nursing a baby. "And that especially was a sad sight," said American Horse.

The influential leader Young Man Afraid of His Horses — which means the *enemy* was afraid of his horses — had been away at the time of the massacre; when he returned he used his considerable influence to quiet things down. He did his best to stop the raiding and skirmishing and, to a degree, succeeded. General Miles, in his turn, made conciliatory sounds; slowly things returned to normal, if anything about reservation life can be said to be normal.

By the middle of January 1891, the

Wounded Knee uprising was over. Many Sioux later claimed that it was men of the 7th Cavalry — Custer's old troop — who started the ferocious firing. They thought the attack was revenge for Custer, who had been defeated and killed fifteen years earlier; many of the descendants of the massacred, as reported in William Coleman's *Voices of Wounded Knee*, certainly believed the 7th was out for revenge that day.

If so, the 7th in this case probably exceeded their mandate. Miles and the other military men could hardly have wanted a massacre — they were well aware that there were thousands of Sioux near Pine Ridge who might go out again and have to be expensively rounded up and subdued.

Meanwhile the power of apprehension did its work. The citizens of communities far away in Nebraska and Iowa fled from what they feared would be the return of terror. Some of these communities were at least 150 miles from the nearest Indian. Mooney considered these panics to be entirely ridiculous.

Not long after the Wounded Knee outbreak a man named Albert Hopkins, who wore a blanket and claimed to be the

Messiah, appeared at Pine Ridge. He claimed the Indians were expecting his arrival, that he acted under what he called "the Pansy Banner of Peace." Besides being the Messiah he was also president of the Pansy Society of America. Red Cloud ridiculed him and had him put off the reservation, but he later surfaced in Washington. He said the Indians would all be waiting for his appearance in the spring, but then he vanished and was heard from no more.

THE

WANING MOON

Though the big historical marker at Wounded Knee claims that the Ghost Dance ended there, in fact it didn't. It was taken up by the Cheyenne, the Arapaho, and other tribes then living in Oklahoma. A second Sitting Bull appeared, this one an Arapaho. A Ghost Dance was held by the Canadian River, near the present-day town of Darlington, Oklahoma: a thousand or more Indians were said to have danced. The Arapaho Sitting Bull instructed all comers: Caddos, Wichitas, and other southern tribes. The local whites were alarmed at first, but the soldiers who came in contact with *this* Sitting Bull found him to be likable and free of humbug — free also of threat.

The dances continued under various leaders — many delegations traveled west to visit Wovoka and receive his instruction — but, in time, most of the tribes who

195

practiced the Ghost Dance lost faith in it. This is not surprising, since none of the things predicted ever came to pass. No new earth formed, no flood swept away the whites. The Paiutes, who had the easiest access to Wovoka, kept dancing longest. There may have been isolated Ghost Dances in northern Arizona as late as 1912; but the failure of the dance to achieve the desired results caused it to be abandoned by most Indians.

Why the Ghost Dance frightened the white authorities so much is still puzzling, and yet it clearly scared them. The fact that Sitting Bull — the Sioux — was doing nothing remotely aggressive didn't save him from death. He failed to stop the Ghost Dance at the whites' request, which he rightly judged to be hypocritical. The whites had *their* dances: why shouldn't Indians have the same right?

Perhaps some whites feared the Ghost Dance because subconsciously they thought it might actually work, at least to the extent of reawakening the warrior instinct in the Sioux. This did happen, but only briefly; wiser heads, such as Young Man Afraid of His Horses, were quick to soothe the situation and prevent more killing.

Long before 1890 the Sioux leaders were well aware that they stood no chance in a shooting war with the American army. Their great victories were a decade and a half behind them. Red Cloud in the north and Quanah Parker in the south did everything they could to ease the difficulties their people felt during this time of transition. Scattered acts of renegadism did occur, but nothing large-scale was ever attempted again.

For a time, though, almost any gathering of Indians, of any size, continued to awaken old fears. When the northern Cheyenne broke out in 1877 the whole of the population of the Great Plains went into a panic. The old apprehension was waiting there in the yeast of pioneer memory; it easily swelled up. In situations such as occurred at Wounded Knee, one shot, accidental or not, was enough to set off one more unnecessary slaughter.

The Great Plains of the American West is a huge space, and yet there proved to be not enough room in it for two races, two ideas of community identity to coexist. Both races, it seemed, needed all the land there in order to survive in their traditional ways. Wounded Knee was a final spasm in the long agony of dispossession.

Black Elk said that he didn't realize at first how much had been lost on that snowy battlefield. In fact, by the time of Wounded Knee, a whole continent had been lost to the native peoples. A process begun in the seventeenth century on the shores of Virginia and Massachusetts got finished on that bleak plain in South Dakota at the ending of the year.

Wounded Knee was not the last conflict between the white government and the native people, but after Wounded Knee the scale changed, and also the methods of dispossession. The latter, since then, has mainly been accomplished through the Congress and the law courts. Chiseling turned out to work as well as shooting. The Five Civilized Tribes in Oklahoma suffered a second dispossession when they were made American citizens — merely a clever ruse to end their system of communal ownership of land. They ceased to be sovereign nations — as brand-new American citizens they were easily cheated.

The white man's appetite for land and profit never slackened: the Indians repeatedly found themselves left with the short end of the stick. Within the last year revelations of large-scale misuse of Indian trust funds have come to light, an indication that this pattern hasn't changed. Large gatherings of Indians are still viewed with suspicion by police, even when Indians are the police. The general attitude seems to be that it cannot be good for too many Indians to assemble, even if they are only getting together for celebration and meditation.

Despite all these losses the native tribes of America still exhibit a good deal of resilience. Some have prospered running casinos — others have managed significant wins in court.

Just over the hill from the Wounded Knee battlefield is Wounded Knee village, a rather cheerful, somewhat suburban community. Someone has taken the trouble to line the highway with vividly painted Drive-Slow signs, urging drivers to remember that there are children at play. The signs insist on responsible driving, and this in a place where most people don't like to drive slow. Wounded Knee, the battlefield, is, like most of the other massacre sites, a somber place; but you only have to go over the hill a few hundred yards to realize that the Sioux are still here and still lively.

History, both ancient and modern,

reminds us that the impulse to turn whole groups of people into meat shops is not likely to be extinguished. Wounded Knee may have been an impulsive massacre, but the others I have considered were not. What happened in Rwanda was not impulsive, either: nor was Saddam's gassing of the Kurds.

Long ago, when I was a young cowboy, I witnessed a herd reaction in a real herd — about one hundred cattle that some cowboys and I were moving from one pasture to another along a small asphalt farm-to-market road. It was mid-afternoon in mid-summer. Men, horses, and cattle were all drowsy, the herd just barely plodding along, until one cow happened to drag her hoof on the rough asphalt, making a loud rasping sound. In an instant that sleepy herd was in full flight, and our horses too. A single sound on a summer afternoon produced a short but violent stampede. The cattle and horses ran full-out for perhaps one hundred yards. It was the only stampede I was ever in, and a dragging hoof caused it.

So it may have been at Wounded Knee. But for Black Coyote's perhaps unintentional shot the old sick chief and his people might merely have grumbled a bit about the disarming and then trundled harmlessly off to Nebraska. But when that shot sounded, the soldiers on the ridge went off like my cows, and, once more, slaughter was unleashed.

A final point about these homely little massacres and the even more terrible ones that keep occurring throughout the world: women and children are almost never exempted. A small anthology could be assembled just of quotations about the desirability of killing the women and children while one is killing undesirables. There one would find John Chivington's "nits breed lice" remarks, and General Sherman's famous grim one-liner.

A star item certainly would be Heinrich Himmler's famous speech delivered in Posen in October of 1943, in which he informed the Nazi hierarchy of the program to exterminate the Jewish people; Himmler himself raises the question of women and children and concludes, after only the briefest pause, that they had better be killed too.

And they were.

This is an old conclusion, many times restated by those inclined to massacre. The earliest statement I have been able to find comes from the prophet Ezekiel, who wrote about 600 B.C.:

> Go yet after him through the city and smite: let not your eye spare, neither have ye pity: slaughter old and young, both maids and little children.
>
> Ezekiel 9:5–6

Time and time across history, Ezekiel's advice has been followed to the letter. The making of meat shops seemingly has no end.

BIBLIOGRAPHICAL

NOTE

The literature on the massacres of the
American West is not really vast, though it
certainly might swell in size if one included
all the memoirs in which one or another of
the massacres is mentioned. This would
include the often homespun recollections
of pioneers, travelers, soldiers, administrators, local historians, newspapermen, (and
women), miners, ministers, railroad men,
cowboys, and the like.

Virtually any of the memoirs might contain a line or two that throws new light on
some aspect of some massacre: perhaps
only a memory, probably inaccurate,
passed down to them from parent or
grandparent.

The genius of Evan Connell's great book
on Custer, *Son of the Morning Star*, is that
he mined just such memoir literature bril-
liantly, constructing around Custer's defeat
a kind of mosaic of local memory, white,

Native American, military, journalistic, and so forth. William Coleman, in *Voices of Wounded Knee*, has done something of the same thing for that encounter.

There is nothing so comprehensive about any of the other massacres in this book. The one study that attempted comprehensiveness, J. P. Dunn's *Massacres of the Mountains*, was published too soon to include Wounded Knee.

The most solid facts about any of these massacres are the dates on which they occurred. All other statements need to be regarded with caution. Will Bagley cheerfully restates this principle in *Blood of the Prophets*, his recent book about Mountain Meadows. The principal fact, in each case, is that a lot of people turned up dead.

How many exactly, and why, is, in almost every case, still disputed.

These are the books I've worked from:

Backus, Anna Jean. *Mountain Meadows Witness: The Life and Times of Bishop Philip Klingensmith.* Arthur H. Clark, 1996.

Bagley, Will. *Blood of the Prophets: Brigham Young and the Massacre at Mountain Meadows.* University of Oklahoma Press, 2002.

Brooks, Juanita. *The Mountain Meadows*

Massacre. University of Oklahoma Press, 1962. The classic account.

Brown, Dee. *Bury My Heart at Wounded Knee.* Holt, Rinehart & Winston, 1970.

Coleman, William. *Voices of Wounded Knee.* University of Nebraska Press, 2000.

Connell, Evan S. *Son of the Morning Star.* Promontory Press, 1993. The illustrated edition.

Cutler, Bruce. *The Massacre at Sand Creek.* University of Oklahoma Press, 1995.

Denton, Sally. *American Massacre: The Tragedy at Mountain Meadows, September 1857.* Knopf, 2003.

Dunn, J. P. *Massacres of the Mountains.* Archer House, 1965.

Hoig, Stan. *The Sand Creek Massacre.* University of Oklahoma Press, 1961.

Jackson, Helen Hunt. *A Century of Dishonor.* Boston, 1881.

Lamar, Howard (ed). *The New Yale Encyclopedia of the American West.* Yale University Press, 1998.

Mendoza, Patrick. *Song of Sorrow: Massacre at Sand Creek.* Willow Wind, 1993.

Mooney, James. *The Ghost-Dance Religion*

and the Sioux Outbreak of 1890. Bureau of American Ethnology, Fourteenth Annual Report, Part II, Washington D.C., 1896.

Roberts, David. *A Newer World: Kit Carson, John Charles Frémont, and the Claiming of the American West.* Simon & Schuster, 2000.

Schellie, Don. *Vast Domain of Blood.* Westernlore, 1968.

Scott, Bob. *Blood at Sand Creek.* Caxton, 1994.

Wilson, James. *The Earth Shall Weep.* Atlantic Monthly Press, 1999.

Wise, William. *Massacre at Mountain Meadows: An American Legend and a Monumental Crime.* Crowell, 1976.

ABOUT
THE AUTHOR

LARRY MCMURTRY is the author of twenty-seven novels, including the Pulitzer Prize–winning *Lonesome Dove*. His other works include two collections of essays, three memoirs, two biographies, and more than thirty screenplays. He lives in Archer City, Texas.

The employees of Thorndike Press hope you have enjoyed this Large Print book. All our Thorndike and Wheeler Large Print titles are designed for easy reading, and all our books are made to last. Other Thorndike Press Large Print books are available at your library, through selected bookstores, or directly from us.

For information about titles, please call:

(800) 223-1244

or visit our Web site at:

www.gale.com/thorndike
www.gale.com/wheeler

To share your comments, please write:

Publisher
Thorndike Press
295 Kennedy Memorial Drive
Waterville, ME   04901